THE COMPANY CHAIRMAN

THE
COMPANY CHAIRMAN

Second Edition

SIR ADRIAN CADBURY

Foreword by Sir John Harvey-Jones

DIRECTOR BOOKS
Published in association with the Institute of Directors

First published 1990

This second edition first published 1995 by
Director Books
an imprint of Fitzwilliam Publishing Limited
Campus 400, Maylands Avenue
Hemel Hempstead
Hertfordshire HP2 7EZ
A division of
Simon & Schuster International Group

The views of the author do not necessarily represent those of the
Council of the Institute of Directors

Typeset in 11/13pt Bembo
by Hands Fotoset, Leicester

Printed and bound in Great Britain by
T.J. Press Ltd, Padstow.

British Library Cataloguing in Publication Data

A catalogue record for this book is available from
the British Library

ISBN 0-13-434150-3

---

1 2 3 4 5   99 98 97 96 95

CONTENTS

FOREWORD

SIR JOHN HARVEY-JONES MBE
Chairman, Parallax Enterprises Limited

Sir Adrian Cadbury and I have long shared a mutual interest in and dedication to the problems of improving our knowledge and skills of the art of chairmanship.

It is a curious fact that this, the top job for people in the business and industrial scene, should seem to command so little attention and interest. In an age when management books, studies, courses and media attention are focused on almost every aspect of the business scene, somehow the qualities required of a chairman, and the attendant role and responsibilities, seem to have been ignored. This may be because, by definition, there are small numbers of chairmen or it may be because it is assumed, quite erroneously, that having reached a level of such distinction there is nothing left for the incumbent to learn.

The fact remains that when a director is asked to take over the responsibilities of chairman he or she is all too often expected to be fully prepared and ready to take on this unique role. That, in many cases, the new chairman succeeds despite this absence of preparation or training is our collective good fortune. But if, as sadly happens from time to time, the novice fails to discharge these responsibilities effectively, the effects are felt by us all, not only within the company, but indirectly within the country, for as a society we depend upon the success of our businesses for the creation of the wealth on which so much else depends.

If a company is successful it is due to the efforts of everyone in it, but if it fails it is because of the failure of the board. If the board fails it is the responsibility of the chairman, notwithstanding the collective responsibility of everyone. Despite this collective responsibility, it is on the chairman's shoulders that the competition and performance of that supreme directing body depends. Our companies and our countries can ill afford failure in the increasingly tough world of international competition. Chairmen cannot win this battle on their own – that depends on the whole team – but they can, and do, sometimes unwittingly create conditions under which even the best of management and work-force are doomed to failure.

Newly appointed chairmen are all too aware of these uncomfortable facts and it is not, therefore, surprising that many seek help and advice from others who practise the art. So far, however, there has been a notable dearth of books written by chairmen, for chairmen, about the exercise of the job. When I was first appointed as a chairman, I studied Hugh Parker's book with the anxiety of a drowning man reaching for a lifebelt. Its practical and safe advice helped me a great deal. There was, however, virtually nowhere else for me to turn at that time. I wish this book had been available when I first took the chair of an industrial organisation. Reading the proofs, despite an unconscious number of years in the chairs of various concerns, I still found much advice and wisdom to help me today, as well as many viewpoints on which to ponder.

While the responsibilities of the chairman do not alter, the role varies with the changing social, economic and political environments in which we operate. Moreover, it behoves the chairman to be aware not only of the massive changes occurring in his or her own company and own country, but also of those which will affect the discharge of his responsibilities that are occurring in Europe as well as in many other parts of the world. There is no company which is immune to the effects of international competition and the changes which are occurring all around us. The chairman reflects the problems and the company. There has never been a time when the task of chairing a public or private company has been more difficult, or when the exercise of skill in that role was more necessary.

As Adrian Cadbury says, there is no textbook solution to these problems, for the role is infinitely variable between companies, countries and times. The fact that the task is not susceptible to precise prescription does not, however, remove from chairmen the need to continuously improve their skills and to learn their craft. The whole time I have served as a chairman I have consciously attempted, every year, to study or learn something which would enable me to become better at my job.

The fact that the chairman's job barely exists within the legal framework does not obviate the fact that boards cannot manage themselves without leadership and help. Every one of us who has served on a committee or a board, or even attended a meeting, knows painfully well the distinction between good and bad leadership from the chair. This involves much more than just getting through the business on time. It is a question of ensuring that a collection of people have the opportunity to air differences, explore ideas, and create the collective views and wisdom which, after all, are the basis of the theory of the leadership of our organisations.

Effective chairmanship is too often the difference between success and failure. It is the performance of this critical catalytic role to which this thoughtful book is dedicated. I, for one, am most grateful to Adrian Cadbury for having written it and have already profited by reading it. I commend it wholeheartedly, not only to those fortunate people who may have the opportunity of becoming a chairman, but to everyone who is interested in this vital area of corporate governance, and that should mean all of us.

ACKNOWLEDGEMENTS

I would like to express grateful thanks to everyone who has helped me with both editions of this book. It began with Fitzwilliam Publications who commissioned the work. It has progressed through to the second edition, thanks to the backing of my publishers and to the patient support of Pat Jennings and Joyce Schofield in preparing the book for publication.

When Fitzwilliam's editor asked me to write about the role of a chairman, the challenge was irresistible. I had often thought about the chairman's task during my time as chairman of a public company, and I have been forever surprised that so little has been written on the subject. Chairmen have to develop their own individual approach to chairmanship, but in so doing they want to test their views against those of their fellow chairmen.

The ideas in the book are not original. They are the result of reading and of observation, and my thanks are due to all the sources on which I have drawn. The opinions expressed are my own and they simply represent one person's assessment of what is involved in chairing a board. Because so many people have contributed, wittingly or otherwise, to these reflections on chairmanship, it is not possible to give credit to everyone from whose advice and example I have benefited.

My main sources have been my colleagues in the company in which I have happily spent my working life. I am greatly indebted to my fellow board members and particularly to the chairmen under whom I have served and from whom I have learnt so much.

The Bank of England and PRO NED have been other important sources of experience and of ideas. Through those institutions, I had the good fortune to work with Sir David Walker and Jonathan Charkham, who have had a marked influence on British thinking on the role of boards and on the relationship between companies and their shareholders. Jonathan Charkham's writings are required reading for any serious student of corporate governance.

In Europe, academic interest in the working of boards is centred on the International Institute for Management Development (IMD) at Lausanne. I have attended their courses and have greatly valued keeping in touch with the Institute's research programme through my links with Dr Ada Demb and Dr F.-Friedrich Neubauer. They have studied company boards in a number of countries and have published their findings in *The Corporate Board: Confronting the Paradoxes*, which presents a fascinating picture of the formal and informal workings of boards of different types in different countries.

I have had the advantage in preparing this edition of my involvement in corporate governance. This has caused me to think more rigorously about board structure and gave me the chance to learn from my colleagues on the governance committee that I chaired. The international interest in corporate governance has, in turn, enabled me to take part in the debate on board issues outside Britain. In this context, my friends in the United States have been particularly helpful in keeping me in touch with American thinking on boards and chairmanship. I owe a particular debt to Robert A. G. Monks for his knowledge and enthusiasm, and to Peter Drucker from whose thinking in this field we all gratefully draw our inspiration.

My final tributes are to Hugh Parker and to Sir John Harvey-Jones. When I first found myself chairman of a board, Hugh Parker gave me invaluable advice as a consultant and as a friend. His book, *Letters to a New Chairman*, remains the standard work on the practical aspects of board chairmanship. We have discussed many of the issues dealt with in this book and he has been an unfailing source of informed comment and of encouragement.

Equally, I am immensely grateful to Sir John Harvey-Jones for writing the foreword. His own book, *Making It Happen*, is the best available account by a chairman of the realities of running a complex, international company. No one in business can fail to learn from reading it. With his support, I hope that the object of writing this book will be achieved. This is that the central importance of the role of the chairman should become more widely recognised.

Sir Adrian Cadbury
January 1995

INTRODUCTION

The aim of this book is to be of practical use to chairmen of companies, whatever their size, and to those who may find themselves asked to take the chair in due course. Although the book is primarily addressed to company chairmen and directors, some of the issues with which it deals are equally relevant to the chairmanship of bodies outside the business sector. For example, the key relationship in a company between the chairman and the chief executive or managing director has its parallels in the governance of clubs, schools and a wide range of voluntary organisations. In discussing the role of company chairmen, the book therefore deals with matters which should be of interest to the chairmen of other types of organisation as well.

One question which needs to be settled at the outset is what title to give to the individual who chairs a board or committee. The straightforward answer is 'chairman', but for fear that this might give the misleading impression that all chairmen are male, two other designations have been brought into use, mainly by public-sector bodies. They are 'chair' and 'chairperson'. The drawback to these two options is that they achieve neutrality of gender at the expense of clear, accepted English.

A useful rule when deciding on job titles in a company is that they should describe as accurately as possible the function which the job-holder carries out. Once a title departs from verbal precision in order to confer status or to meet an individual's self-esteem, an element of confusion is brought into the company structure. This is likely to cause misunderstandings in time both within and without the organisation.

On the basis of that rule, I exclude the word 'chair' because it confuses the person with the office, quite apart from lending itself to such infelicitous compounds as 'vice-chair'. There is well-established authority for the use of the word chair for the post of a professor, or

1

for the seat of office. In the latter sense you can take the chair, or put someone in the chair, but the chair is the position of authority, not the person who is sitting in it.

'Chairperson' has a better claim than 'chair' to be considered as an alternative to chairman and it is beginning to make its way into dictionaries. It is, however, a contrived word and its awkwardness becomes apparent when you attempt to use it in the plural to describe, say, deputy chairmen.

I come back, therefore, to the word 'chairman' because, leaving aside the seventeenth century use of the word for someone whose occupation was to wheel bath-chairs, its dictionary definition is both established and precise:

> The occupier of a chair of authority; the person chosen to preside over
> a meeting, a company, a corporate body, etc. (*Shorter OED* 1975)

It is clear from this definition that the occupier of the chair can be a woman or a man and it is in that sense that chairmen are referred to throughout the book. I make that point, because I regard it as of the first importance that the scales should not appear to be further loaded against women in the male-dominated world of British business; British companies would gain from having more women as board members, which would in turn lead to the appointment of more women as chairmen. In the meantime, anyone who thinks that the term 'chairman' excludes women has only to consult the dictionary.

I began by saying that the book aims to be helpful to those involved with the running of companies, whatever their size. This point needs to be made, given my background as a former chairman of a large public limited company. But the Cadbury business was still mainly family owned and managed when I joined it, and its board met weekly and operated far more as a management committee than it did as a true company board. I have, therefore, had direct experience of the transition from a family firm to a publicly quoted company, and from that to the international business which was formed by the merger between Cadbury and Schweppes in 1969. It is in those transitional stages from the small to the medium-sized business and from the latter to the large organisation that the guiding hand of the chairman is so critical.

If the question of chairmanship is important to small and medium-sized companies, the same holds equally for large and well-managed organisations. It might be thought that the role of the chairman in a company like Imperial Chemical Industries would have become so clearly established that an incoming chairman would simply carry on where his predecessor left off. However, as Sir John Harvey-Jones makes clear in his admirable book *Making It Happen*, the chairman's task needs to be redefined by each new incumbent.

When he became chairman of ICI, Sir John took the executive members of his board away for a week to discuss how the board was to work together to give the company the lead for which it was looking. This was necessary because the relationship between a board and its chairman changes when a new appointment to the chair is made. The board of ICI had to review its role in the light of the challenges which were then facing the company and this in turn helped to define what was expected of their chairman. There is, therefore, a continual need to rethink and reappraise the interlocking tasks of chairmen and of their boards, which is one reason why it is logical for chairmen to be appointed for an agreed term of office.

Where the chairmen of large organisations do have an advantage is that they are less likely to face change of the same order as that which confronts companies, as they move across the decisive boundaries which separate small, medium-sized and large businesses. In addition, such chairmen have more resources to call on and people to consult in deciding how their roles should alter to meet changes in the competitive climate. There are, of course, management consultants who specialise in the work of boards and who are in a position to draw on their experience to help chairmen of companies determine how they can best contribute to the success of their enterprises. Apart from professional consultants, what other sources of advice are open to chairmen, whatever the size of their company?

There is a good deal of written guidance as to the duties of directors, and all directors should be aware of their considerable responsibilities from the moment that they join a board. The Institute of Directors publishes a number of up-to-date and informative books on the responsibilities of directors, but there is little which has been written specifically on the role of the chairman, except for Hugh Parker's *Letters to a New Chairman* which I have found invaluable. The reasons why the post of chairman has received little formal attention will be discussed in the opening chapter, but, as a result, the reading list of British or American books addressed to chairmen or aspiring chairmen is short.

How, then, do chairmen learn about chairmanship, whether as chairmen of companies or chairmen of committees and bodies outside the company sector? In the main, chairmen learn from their experience of being chaired and of taking the chair. As so often, we are expected to pick up whatever we need to know as we go along.

This casual approach to the training of chairmen seems all the more odd when you reflect on the importance of the role.

When we attend a meeting of any kind, we can sense almost from the start whether the chairman is competent or not. Provided he or she is, then the time spent in discussion will be well spent and the meeting will have served a useful purpose. If the chairman is not up to the task, it is improbable that the meeting will achieve anything except the frustration of those attending, who will have wasted that most precious of resources – their time. The quality of chairmanship is the key to the success or failure of a meeting, which suggests that far more thought needs to be given to the best ways of preparing people for the role of chairman.

Interestingly enough, Britain would appear to have something of a comparative advantage as a source of competent chairmen for international organisations, in spite of showing little concern for how they should be trained. The longest-serving administrator in Brussels told me that Community officials welcomed Britons taking the chair at European meetings, because they exercised the discipline which was needed to reach conclusions, while ensuring that essential differences of view were properly aired. I have heard similar views expressed in the United States about British chairmanship of bodies concerned with international finance.

The straightforward explanation for this apparent facility for chairmanship is that it is the result of practice in the art, given the reliance which is placed in Britain on the committee approach. The facility may also have been encouraged by an educational system which was geared, in the nineteenth century, to the education of efficient administrators of the British Empire. Much of an administrator's work involved, in effect, acting as chairman and ruling on issues which could be resolved only after listening to detailed debates and carefully weighing up the available evidence. Certainly the qualities required of chairmen, such as even-handedness, willingness to listen and the ability to control a meeting, are ones which have traditionally been rated highly in this country.

I first found myself in the chair at meetings when I was at school and at university; looking back, this gave me useful experience and the chance to make mistakes when their consequences were not serious. At that age, too, you receive instant and blunt feedback from your fellows, without which it is difficult to know how to improve. One of the points which Sir John Harvey-Jones makes well in his book is the need for board members to help their chairmen by telling them frankly what they have handled well, what badly and why. Without that kind of constructive response from below the chair, it is hard for chairmen to improve their chairmanship.

After starting work, I had some useful lessons in chairmanship from serving on various company joint consultative bodies and later from chairing them myself. Unlike boards, joint consultative bodies do not form a single constituency with a single purpose. They are made up of representatives of different interests and it is the chairman's job to help those representatives find enough common ground to make progress. This calls for just those qualities of impartiality and willingness to listen to which I have already referred, plus the ability to know when and how to give the committee a lead.

Another benefit from serving on joint consultative bodies is that trade union representatives are usually better versed in the rules and procedures of committees than their management counterparts. It is a necessary part of the job of chairmen to know what is or is not in order at any particular meeting. They have to be able to distinguish between the invoking of rules in order to obstruct and doing so in order to keep the discussion on the rails. They also have to learn to appreciate the importance of minutes – usually the hard way, by finding that imprecise or inaccurate wording in the record of one meeting leads to continuing difficulties at subsequent meetings. Once the minutes of a meeting have been accepted as a true record, they are understandably hard to rewrite.

My most memorable lessons in the art of chairmanship came from serving at an early stage in my career on two outside bodies. One was the Cambridge University Appointments Board, whose chairman was Sir Frank Lee. He was a distinguished civil servant and had been Permanent Secretary at the Board of Trade. The Appointments Board was a mixed bag of academics and of representatives from business, with some ready talkers on it. Sir Frank was a masterly chairman; he ensured that everyone who had anything constructive to say said it, while at the same time keeping us all strictly to the point. The lesson I learnt from him was the importance of being crystal-clear as to the aim of the meeting and then of holding everyone to that aim.

The other body, which I joined in 1962, was the Commonwealth Immigrants Advisory Board. I suspect I was put on it in mistake for some more senior member of my family, but if so it was a fortunate error from my point of view, because the Board's chairman was Lady Reading. She was an exceptionally able and experienced chairman and taught me the importance of thorough preparation before taking the chair at a meeting. I have already said that it is important for a chairman to listen, but that alone is not enough – it is important to know what to listen *for*. It is only by studying the papers beforehand and thinking in advance about the issues which are on the agenda, that the chairman will be able to make the best use of the committee's time and to know what questions should be raised and answered in the course of the meeting. All the Board's reports were, unusually, published as White Papers, so there were further useful lessons to be learnt about the chairman's role in drafting papers and in winning the confidence and co-operation of those who were summoned to give evidence to the Board.

In 1991 I became chairman of the Committee on the Financial Aspects of Corporate Governance, which was set up to recommend a Code of Best Practice for listed companies registered in the United Kingdom. I was fortunate in the membership of the Committee and in the nature of its task, because we were dealing with issues in which I had an abiding interest. Chairing a committee which is charged with agreeing any set of guidelines for conduct is difficult enough, but doubly so when they concern such an elusive and contentious subject as corporate governance.

My involvement with matters of corporate governance in Britain and internationally has reinforced my views on the crucial nature of the chairman's role. It is important to design board systems which incorporate an appropriate structure of checks and balances; how effective they are, however, depends primarily on the chairman. That is one reason why, in this second edition, I have given a whole chapter to the question of whether there are two jobs or one at the head of a company.

Two of the commonest criticisms of our Committee's conclusions have been that we should have made the split between the chairman and the chief executive mandatory for publicly quoted companies and that the stress we put on the role of the non-executive directors would undermine the unitary nature of British boards. Both are matters which I discuss further in the book and both bear directly on the role of the chairman.

I should make it clear at this point that I have no special credentials for writing on the subject of chairmanship. The experience of any one individual is necessarily limited, and so I have aimed to supplement that experience through reading what I can about the chairman's role and through discussing it with other chairmen. Equally, I have looked at the chairman's job from the point of view of the way I think it should be done, rather than the way I did it myself. All I can claim is to have given a good deal of thought to the question of chairmanship and I remain astonished that such an important and fascinating subject appears to have been so little researched or written about.

Turning now from background to the book itself, it is in no sense a management textbook. The role of a chairman varies as a company grows and changes; it will vary even more between companies. Equally, the way in which the role is carried out will depend on the personality of each individual chairman and on the personalities of his or her colleagues. There can be no universal job description for a chairman. What is possible, however, is to draw attention to a number of issues, which most chairmen will have to resolve in deciding how they intend to discharge their role – the role for which their fellow board or committee members have selected them.

CHAPTER 1

THE CHAIRMAN'S
CHANGING ROLE

> But the chairman is the chairman of the board. He is not
> chairman of the company. There is no such position as
> chairman of the company.
> Geoffrey Mills, *Controlling Companies*

THE LEGAL POSITION OF THE CHAIRMAN

Geoffrey Mills' definition of the position of the chairman is technically
correct. The chairman is the person whom the board elects to take the
chair at a particular meeting. The board is not bound to continue with
the same chairman for successive meetings and is entitled to choose
whomsoever it wants, from among its members, as chairman. In law,
all directors have equal responsibilities and the chairman is no more
equal than any other board member. Chairmen are an administrative
convenience and a means of ensuring that board meetings are properly
conducted.

Since their role is not legally recognised, chairmen are barely
mentioned in Britain's Companies Acts. Section 6 of the 1967 Act
does lay down that the chairman's emoluments should be disclosed
in the company's annual accounts and the chairman's signature is
required on certain formal documents. Those precepts apart, the only
other statutory requirement of chairmen is that they should be on
time, if they want to retain their positions. For example, the Articles
of Association of Cadbury Schweppes have this to say about how the
chair should be taken at a General Meeting of the company:

> The Chairman of the Board, if any, or in his absence the Deputy
> Chairman of the Board, if any, shall preside as Chairman at every
> General Meeting, but if there be no such Chairman or Deputy
> Chairman, or if neither of them be present within ten minutes after the

time appointed for holding the meeting, or shall decline to take or shall retire from the chair, the Directors present shall choose one of their number to act as Chairman of such meeting, and if there be no Director chosen who shall be willing to act, the members present in person and entitled to vote shall choose one of their own number to act as Chairman at such meeting.

This is a tighter timetable than that suggested in Table A of the Companies Acts, which is a cogent reason for reading your own company's articles carefully. Cadbury Schweppes has a similar article covering ordinary board meetings, but there the leeway given to the chairman is only five minutes, after which time the board chooses one of those present to chair the meeting. So from a statutory point of view there is no need for a company to have a continuing chairman and the law is solely concerned with a chairman's pay and punctuality.

In effect, the Companies Acts are framed to ensure that someone takes the chair, but they are not concerned with who does so. The chairmanship could, for example, rotate among board members, just as in former days all directors of the Bank of England could expect in turn to become Governor. The law looks on the post of chairman as one which is exercised meeting by meeting; the outside world sees the chairman as the head of the company. The gap between the legal and the established role of the chairman is exemplified by this difference of view as to the importance and relative permanence of the chairman; the two of course go together.

DEVELOPMENT OF THE CHAIRMAN'S POSITION

Companies more in the public eye

Why has the position of chairman acquired greater significance, particularly in the eyes of the outside world, since I first became chairman of a publicly quoted company thirty years ago? The main reason is that the pace of business activity has become more hectic and the public attention focused on companies has become greater.

The debate on corporate governance, for example – on the system by which companies are directed and controlled – is now worldwide. It came to public attention in Britain after the Committee on the Financial Aspects of Corporate Governance had been set up in 1991. The Committee was asked to address the lack of confidence in financial reports and accounts and in the audit statements attached to them, against a background of some well-publicised failures of prominent companies, whose published statements appeared to give no forewarning of the disasters to come. These concerns over reporting standards were heightened by subsequent episodes such as the collapse of the BCCI Bank, the Maxwell affair and the continuing controversy over directors' pay. They put corporate governance on the front page and drew attention to the fundamental governance issues, which centre on the effectiveness and accountability of boards of directors. Given that chairmen have the prime responsibility for the conduct of their boards, they in their turn became the focus of attention.

It is not, however, only the downside of business activity which has drawn attention to the role of boards and thereby of their chairmen. Companies have grown larger and more international and have extended the range of goods and services that they supply. Their growth has involved bids and mergers on an increasing scale. The public is now only too conscious of the impact which such events as takeovers, closures and the ups and downs of trade in general can have on their lives.

Bids and counterbids are dramatic events in themselves; all the more so when they cross national boundaries and involve sums which are equivalent to the national debts of smaller sovereign-states. In addition, the well-publicised transgressions of a few individual businessmen and some long-running battles between certain companies have all made exciting copy. Thus more space is now given to business news in the press and on radio and television, and business is far more in the public eye than it used to be.

To bring these business sagas to life, commentators choose to describe them in terms of the personalities involved. It is a way of simplifying often complex issues and meeting the brief spans of attention allotted to them by the media. When a company is in the news, the spotlight of publicity is thus focused on the chairman as the personification of the company, with one or two notable exceptions such as Lord Weinstock, who has headed the General Electric Company in Britain as managing director since 1963. Chairmen have, therefore, become more visible and this is understandable given that they are usually responsible for the external relations of the companies whose boards they chair. It does, however, tend to exaggerate the significance of the chairman's position, since it is the board as a team which is responsible for a company's policies and decisions. The same shift has occurred in the political world where, due largely to the power of television, the focus is increasingly on individual politicians rather than on the parties which they represent.

All of this is not just true of large companies, which may regularly be the centre of media attention. Whatever the size of a company, when it is in the news, it is to the chairman that the reporters will turn. In these circumstances it is essential that the company should speak with a single voice and the voice will normally be that of the chairman.

Wider shareholding

It is not only the dramas of business life which have propelled chairmen into a prominence which they would mostly prefer to avoid. Many more people in Britain have now become shareholders, through the privatisation of major public-sector companies, the growth in employee share ownership schemes and, to an extent, through management buy-outs as well. The paradox is that the number of shareholders in the population has grown rapidly in the last few years, while the proportion of the shares of most public limited companies held by individuals has fallen dramatically over a rather longer period. Their place has been taken by institutional investors, such as pension funds and insurance companies. The effect, however, of the rise of the institutional investor and of the move to wider share ownership has been to increase the demand for information on companies and on their activities.

Since it is the chairman who reports the company's annual and half-yearly results, it is to the chairman that those who have an interest in company affairs look for enlightenment between these announcements. This in itself raises difficult issues, which will be discussed later, over what information should be given on the state of the business, and to whom, outside these twice-yearly events. The direct result, however, of a wider interest in the progress of companies is that the chairmen of their boards are now subject to greater attention from financial analysts and commentators.

Business and the community

Chairmen come to the attention of the public not simply in connection with the financial results of their companies, but in relation to their companies' social role as well. Companies are now expected to play a more direct part in community affairs and to assist, for example, in a variety of training and education initiatives, in bringing new life back into inner-city areas and in improving the environment. These are all activities which are of interest to an audience beyond those who follow the fortunes of companies. They are, also, likely to raise contentious issues at times and so they push companies willy-nilly into the political arena.

On an even wider front, the general public are now more inclined to communicate directly with chairmen to express their views. Consumer journals, the advice columns of magazines and pressure groups all recommend writing to the chairman as the best way of obtaining a satisfactory response from a company; some even provide lists of names and addresses to speed such missives on their way. I have seen a marked increase in the letters which I received from the public during my time as chairman. By no means all are complaints, many are appeals for help and reflect an overestimation of the powers of those in business to influence the world beyond their companies. They are further evidence of the increased visibility of chairmen.

Development of the chairman's role

To conclude this section on the way in which the chairman's role has developed, it is entirely correct to say that chairmen are chairmen only of their boards and not of their companies – correct but misleading. Misleading because, in reality and in the eyes of the world, chairmen have become chairmen of their companies and not simply of their boards. The position of chairman has no particular *legal* significance, but it has acquired *public* significance.

Where I think that the chairman's lack of legal standing does have consequences is that it helps to explain why the role of the chairman has been largely overlooked by management researchers and writers. Given that the chairman's position has no basis in law and that it is exercised in different ways in different companies, it has been felt to be too individual a matter for general conclusions to be drawn about it. This to me is a serious omission, because even with these limitations, there is much to be gained by analysing the chairman's job, given the importance which I believe should be attributed to it.

THE CHAIRMAN'S BOARD RESPONSIBILITIES

This takes us straight into the question of the function which the chairman performs. Since this is in effect the subject of the book, what is needed at the outset is a general picture of what is expected of company chairmen. This will set the scene and provide a frame-work which can be filled in with more detail in later chapters. As I explained in the introduction, I use the word 'chairman' throughout in its dictionary sense to include men and women equally.

Less accurately, I refer to a chairman in the singular as 'he', simply because of the limitations of the English language in this regard and because the continual repetition of 'he or she' becomes wearisome. I have used the same shorthand in referring to directors and other executives. It is, nevertheless, important to keep 'he or she' in mind as more women become directors and chairmen of companies.

Another point which has already been touched on is that the role of a chairman is a personal one. It will vary with individual chairmen, with the boards for which they are responsible, with the companies involved and with the stage of development through which they are moving. There is no straightforward job description to which chairmen can work. Chairmen have to decide for themselves just what they are able to do for their boards and their companies which no one else can do and just what it is that their boards expect of them. The aim of this book is to promote more discussion about the different aspects of the chairman's role and the ways in which they can be carried out. It is for individual chairmen to judge which of the issues thus raised are relevant as far as they are concerned and what personal balance to strike between the different duties which chairmen undertake.

Board leadership

The basic responsibility of chairmen is to ensure that their boards are effective and that they are giving their companies the lead that they need. I start with board leadership, because too many descriptions of the duties of directors and of boards focus on their monitoring role. This presupposes that the business drive comes from the managers of a company and that the board is there primarily to keep them on the rails. It is for the board, representing the interests of those who appoint them, to set the standards which they expect from the managers and to set them high. It is the chairman's job to see that the board provides the company with leadership and gives it a sense of vision. The board drives and encourages as well as checks.

Board membership

The board can only give the necessary lead if it has the right balance of membership. It is thus part of the chairman's agenda to keep a watch on the overall size of the board, on the balance between outside or non-executive directors and inside or executive directors, and on the balance of age, experience and personalities around the board table. Since the circumstances facing companies are continually changing, the composition of their boards will need to alter over time in response to changes in the competitive environment. The chairman is responsible for the process of renewal, which is essential to the maintenance of an effective board.

Board direction

Given a board which has the right balance of membership and has accepted its leadership role, it is up to the chairman to see that it concentrates on directing the company and not on attempting to manage it. It is the board's responsibility to determine the aims of the company and to decide on the strategy, plans and policies for carrying out those aims. This is the job of *direction*, which the board alone can do and on which it needs to focus its attention. There is a natural temptation for boards to stray from the more abstract issues of direction to the more hands-on issues of management, particularly if things are not going according to plan. Management issues are more immediate and easier to get to grips with than questions of strategy. But the board has appointed managers to turn its decisions into action and it must allow them to do so. Chairmen need to preserve the distinction between the role of the board and the role of the management as rigorously as they can.

Board monitoring

The next two tasks follow on directly from the last one. Having set aims and targets, the board needs to check that it is on course for achieving them. If unanticipated events have occurred, as they are bound to from time to time, are the appropriate actions being taken in response? Here again, the chairman has to ensure that the way in which the board monitors progress does not spill over into intervening in the management of the business. Nevertheless, in an increasingly litigious world, boards must be seen to be fulfilling their supervisory role on behalf of the shareholders with due diligence.

Responsibility for people

The board has a similar responsibility in respect of the people at the top of the company. The board has to satisfy itself that the right individuals are in the right jobs and that the senior management of the company as a whole is of the necessary calibre. This is an especially important responsibility when companies are growing rapidly. Chairmen should know the senior executives who are already in place and as much as possible about their potential successors. It is part of their job to see that the human resources of the company are regularly reviewed by the board.

Provision of information

In addition, chairmen have the task of preparing for and chairing the meetings of their boards. I will have more to say later on the chairing of meetings, but one essential aspect of the chairman's responsibilities is to make sure that board members have relevant, up-to-date information on the progress of the company. They need this if they are to carry out their directorial duties competently. No board can function effectively without timely and appropriate information.

Summary of responsibilities

I would summarise the responsibilities of chairmen to their boards as being to ensure the following:

- that the board provides leadership and vision;
- that the board has the right balance of membership;
- that the board sets the aims, strategy and policies of the company;
- that the board monitors the achievement of those aims;
- that the board reviews the resources of people in the company;
- that the board has the information it needs for it to be effective.

There is one further responsibility of a somewhat different kind which needs to be added to that list. Boards on the whole meet monthly at the most, and important decisions which would normally involve the board may have to be taken between meetings. Here chairmen have the task of standing in for the board. It will be for them to judge whether they can speak for the board on their own authority, or whether they need to consult other board members before coming to a decision. Either way, chairmen are the link between the board and the executive directors between board meetings and as a result they need to be readily available to their executive colleagues.

The responsibilities which I have listed are those relating to the chairmanship of the board, because the basic task of all chairmen is to be responsible for their boards. How much in addition they undertake, for example in representing their companies externally, will depend on the time they give to the chairmanship and whether the jobs of chairman and chief executive are separate or not. What is clear from the list is that the role of the chairman and the role of the board are interdependent. Chairmen are responsible for the way in which their boards work, but boards are responsible for whom they have as chairmen.

Chairman's check-list

As a check on my list of a chairman's responsibilities, I append the one drawn up by Juran and Louden and quoted by Sir Walter Puckey in his book, *The Board-Room*:

Apply rules of order.
Decide who has floor.
Proper sequence of business.
What is state of motions.
Stimulate board discussion.
Helps latter to stay objective in good humour.
Identifies misunderstandings.
Guides members in clearing up.
Alert to discover when 'sense of meeting' reached.
Responsibility to convene board meeting.
Plan schedule of meeting.
Arrange and prepare agenda.
Advance information package.
Minutes.
Supervise secretary.
He has the responsibility to:
1. Give leadership to the board on policy formation.
2. Give guidance to the board on distinguishing between board problems and management problems.
3. Provide liaison between the board and the outside directors between meetings.
4. Provide liaison between board and C.E.O., in and between meetings. Follow up to see that board decisions are acted on.
5. Nominate committees of board.
6. Review the performance of the board.
7. Has the responsibility of a director asking questions, making proposals, 'voting'.

(Puckey 1969, p.107)

It is an odd mixture of administrative details and broad responsibilities, but it covers much the same ground as my list, with more emphasis on the actual task of chairing a meeting. It omits any reference to people, either as board members or as top managers, which I regard as an important aspect of the chairman's job. It does, however, introduce a responsibility which I did not include specifically, namely that of reviewing the performance of the board; this is a useful addition. I did say that chairmen were responsible for the effectiveness of their boards, but the concept of reviewing how well they are working sharpens that point up. There is no one other than the chairman who can put such a review in hand.

THE CHAIRMAN'S EXTERNAL RESPONSIBILITIES

Up until now the responsibilities of the chairman that we have been considering are those directly related to the work of the board; they are responsibilities which are internal to the company. Most chairmen, however, have an external role to play as well, as has already been discussed. Chairmen are the link with the shareholders through their written communications with them and through their chairing of the Annual General Meeting. It is a logical extension of these responsibilities to the shareholders that they should also be responsible for the company's relationships with other outside groups. In their representational role, chairmen speak for the board, which in turn implies that they are always close enough to their board's thinking to know how to respond on its behalf to issues which may emerge without notice.

Reporting financial results

Among the chairmen's external responsibilities, the most clear-cut are those which relate to reporting on the financial state of the business. It is for chairmen in their statements to shareholders and at the Annual General Meeting to indicate how the company is progressing. It is prudent for there to be only one source of information about the company's prospects and for that source to be the chairman. In practice, finance directors and chief executives may well talk to financial analysts and commentators more often than their chairmen, but in doing so they are acting on their behalf and chairmen have delegated their authority to them for this purpose. If the market is misled about how the company is faring or if conflicting views about its prospects are being expressed from within the business, then it is the chairman who will be held responsible. It is the chairman who is accountable to the shareholders for the financial state of the company.

The wider representational role

In addition to reporting on the company's progress and prospects to shareholders and to the financial community, the chairman normally has a wider representational role. It is for the chairman to put across the company's aims and policies to all those whose confidence in the business is important. They include those who provide the company with finance and individual major investors. Chairmen need, as well, to maintain good contacts with government, with Members of Parliament and civil servants who have an interest in the company, with the appropriate industry associations and with relevant bodies involved in public affairs.

Having a range of outside contacts provides chairmen with ways of keeping up with good business practice in countries other than their own. For example, committees of the board have been more formally developed in the United States than elsewhere and are gradually becoming an accepted part of the board structure in other countries. I would expect chairmen to be aware of developments of this kind and to examine how far they could be drawn on in their companies to improve board effectiveness. The responsibility of chairmen for external relations includes picking up signals or ideas from the outside world, which could be put to use for the benefit of the company.

The role of guardian

Another aspect of the chairman's responsibility for the public face of the company is as guardian of its character and conduct. The standards in a company are set from the top. It is for the chairman and the board to ensure that everyone in their business knows what the company stands for and what standards of conduct are expected from them. It is also their responsibility to see that those standards are lived up to. It is not enough to pass pious resolutions at the board; what matters is making sure that they are adhered to down the line. That is why if anyone in a company acts improperly, the ultimate responsibility rests with the chairman.

The role of arbiter

Following on from the role of chairmen as guardians of the company's good name, it may fall to them to act as arbiter or umpire over disputes that have arisen internally or externally. They are more likely to be called upon to act in this way if they are not doubling up as chief executives. This is because the kind of issues which are likely to end up on the chairman's desk are those where an executive decision is being challenged either from within the company by an aggrieved employee, or from outside the company by a dissatisfied consumer, customer or supplier.

People, generally, have an innate sense of fairness and if they feel that they have been unjustly dealt with, they will press their suit as far as they possibly can. Provided chairmen have not been involved in the decision which is felt to be unfair, they can look at the facts with reasonable impartiality and may often be able to settle, without rancour, problems which might otherwise have led to a public row or to litigation. No chairman wants to have to make these kinds of judgements, but the ability to do so is a modest argument in favour of the chairman standing outside the executive line of authority.

A different aspect of the same role is that board members may from time to time wish to discuss their personal problems with the chairman. Again, the more independent chairmen are of the executive line, the more helpful they can be as a source of impartial advice. Board members may not, however, always come to the chairman when difficulties arise between them, and here chairmen need to be aware of the feelings of their individual board colleagues and to be prepared to help resolve potential conflicts. A wise and approachable company doctor, in the medical rather than the receiver's sense, may be just as useful as the chairman in this regard. Such a person would have the added advantage of being someone whom chairmen themselves could consult into the bargain.

WHAT MANNER OF CHAIRMAN?

Having briefly reviewed the full range of responsibilities of the chairman, I now turn to some of the ways in which those responsibilities can be discharged. The manner in which chairmen approach their jobs will depend on their individual temperament and on how they and their boards define the chairman's role. There are, however, some commonly used distinctions to describe different types of chairmanship, such as between those who are solely chairmen and those who are chairmen and chief executives, between full- and part-time chairmen and between executive and non-executive chairmen.

Chairman and chief executive

The most unambiguous definition of the chairman's role is when it is combined with that of chief executive. The chairman is then clearly executive, clearly full-time and responsible both for the work of the board and for the management of the company. There are advantages and disadvantages to this combination, but from a definitional point of view there can be no doubt about the role and responsibilities of the person who holds both posts.

Full-time or part-time?

When the top job is divided into two, then the definition of the chairman's role becomes less precise. The one firm plank to which a definition can be nailed is the amount of time chairmen spend on their company's business. This will to a great extent determine their relationship with their chief executives. A full-time chairman is likely to assume the broad range of internal and external responsibilities which have already been outlined. Chairmen who divide their time between more than one company could be expected to retain their responsibilities for the board and its work, but to share the external role with their chief executives.

Chairmen may only spend part of their time with a particular company, but it is misleading to refer to them as part-time chairmen. They remain chairmen of their boards and companies irrespective of the day of the week or the time of day. This is why the American term 'outside chairman' is a more accurate description of their role.

In the same way, a full-time chairman is more likely than a chairman who holds other posts to be an insider, in the sense of someone who has made his career in the company. The combination of knowledge of the business and of the chairmanship being their main occupation is likely to lead full-time insider chairmen to become thoroughly involved in the affairs of their companies. The essential corollary is that they and their chief executives should be clearly agreed on their respective roles.

Executive or non-executive?

I regard the time distinction as being useful in defining what a chairman actually does in a company, whereas it is much harder to pin down precisely what the words 'executive' or 'non-executive' mean when applied to the chairman's role. Since the titles 'executive chairman' and 'non-executive chairman' are commonly used, it is important to try and clarify what the word 'executive' signifies in this context.

In its most straightforward sense, the term 'executive' means having the executive authority to put decisions into effect. Executives, therefore, have people who report to them and to whom they can give instructions. By that test, I was a non-executive chairman of Cadbury Schweppes, since the only person directly responsible to me was my secretary and it was the chief executive who issued all the operating orders. I had a functional or 'dotted-line' relationship with the company secretary and with the finance director in order to fulfil my responsibilities for the work of the board and for the financial state of the business; but they both reported managerially to the chief executive.

Although I was non-executive in the sense of not issuing management instructions of any kind, I do not think that the label 'non-executive' would have been helpful either internally or externally. My main job was as chairman of the company in which I had spent my working life and so I carried more responsibility for the business than the tag 'non-executive' would have implied.

The root of the problem is that to describe either chairmen or directors as non-executive does not convey at all clearly what their role is and what it is that they do. This is partly because the definition is negative and limits itself to what the job is not, rather than to what it is. More fundamentally, it conveys the impression that to be non-executive is to be toothless, to have no power or authority. This is a misunderstanding, because chairmen may not have managerial authority – and indeed normally will not have if they are working with a chief executive – but that does not mean that they are without authority. Chairmen have the authority of the board for whom they speak, rather than managerial authority. The source of their authority is, therefore, different from that of the executives, whose authority derives from the jobs to which they have been appointed.

Another way of getting to grips with the question of whether chairmen are executive or not is to define the word 'executive' rather differently, as Sir Walter Puckey does in *The Board-Room*:

> The term executive implies direct accountability for achieving certain specific tasks and I have no doubt that a chairman has a very considerable *direct* accountability for some very important ones including the fact that he is finally accountable for the efficiency of the board. Therefore even if a chairman is not wholly occupied in the company, he has executive accountabilities in it. (p. 104)

I do not find his definition of executive entirely convincing, but I agree with the conclusion. It confirms the view expressed to me more than once in such comments as, 'There is no such thing as a non-executive chairman.' Indeed, J. G. Beevor in his useful booklet *The Effective Board* (1975, p. 10) states, 'No chairman is wholly non-executive.' Sir Walter Puckey's statement of accountability seems to me to convey what the chairman's job entails more accurately than descriptions which are based on a narrow view of what constitutes executive authority.

Heidrick and Struggles published a survey in 1987 which on page 12 provides further confirmation of the imprecise way in which chairmen are described:

> 'Non executive chairman', 'executive chairman', 'chairman and chief executive' – different titles but do they in fact signify different and separate responsibilities? Our survey showed that titles can be very misleading. Many of those chairmen surveyed who are acknowledged to run very successful companies and are thought to be non executive are anything but that. We found that they are either plainly or overtly regarded as executive by their subordinates or they are in effect the chief executive because of the degree of control they exercise over the nominated chief executive.
>
> Even in the very large companies where the appointment of the chairman is handled through long-established and formal procedures, we found that the chairmen are fully executive in all but name.
>
> We also found a similar, but reversed, position in those companies which genuinely had a non executive or part time chairman. In those circumstances, and in the overwhelming majority of cases, the chief executive was in effect the executive chairman.

These conclusions seem to me to be too sweeping, since there has to be a fundamental difference between combining and dividing the jobs of chairman and chief executive, even taking into account that different individuals will split the work between them differently. What I find important about that passage is that it brings out how much confusion there is about the role of the chairman and the way it should be described. The object of attaching labels to the chairman's title is to clarify their position to those in the company and to those outside it. If those labels then turn out to be misleading or plain inaccurate, it is better to drop them.

My conclusion is that there are two distinctions which matter, by which I mean that they convey useful information to all concerned about the chairman's role in any particular company. The first is whether the jobs of the chairman and the chief executive are separate or combined, and the second is whether chairmen spend all or part of their time with their companies. I believe that chairmen should be referred to as chairmen and that to designate them as executive or non-executive adds nothing of value.

HOW THE CHAIRMAN'S ROLE HAS DEVELOPED

In the United Kingdom and the Commonwealth

Having outlined the responsibilities of the chairman, we return to the question of how they have been affected by the greater attention which is now paid to companies and to their affairs. Companies in this country have moved more into the public eye because of the influence which they are seen as having over the economy, because their activities have become more newsworthy through bids and buy-outs and because they have become more involved in community affairs. In part, the greater influence currently accorded to business reflects the reduced influence which governments are now generally seen to be able to exercise over the economy.

The ability of governments to control the economy has probably never been as real as it has appeared to be to politicians. But apart from recognising the limits to their influence more clearly, governments in the western world have on the whole drawn back from detailed intervention in economic decisions. They have concentrated instead on the role – which is theirs alone – of putting in place the economic framework within which companies can then take their own decisions. This swing from the attempt to control from the centre to a reliance on market forces has been particularly marked in Britain.

Now that companies are perceived as having more power to affect the nature and the level of economic activity, so those who are thought to run them have found themselves becoming public figures. Chairmen have traditionally held a special place in the business hierarchy in Britain, just as chief executives have in the United States. Britain also has more quoted companies than other European countries and these companies report regularly and openly on their activities. Thus in Britain and in those countries, mainly in the Commonwealth, which follow the same boardroom pattern, the role of the chairman has become more prominent and chairmen themselves more publicly visible. This has not just meant that they have had to be more willing to appear on television or to give interviews, it has added to the substance of the chairman's role both internally and externally.

Within their companies, chairmen are responsible for the work of their boards. The more they are expected to speak for their boards and to act for them between board meetings, the more they come to represent the board and to become accountable for its actions. As a consequence, chairmen need to be involved in those decisions, in support of which they may be called upon to speak. Further, it is likely to mean that the part they play in those decisions will become greater. If chairmen are to present their company's position effectively, they will need to know how that position was arrived at and it helps if they are broadly in sympathy with it.

By the same token, chairmen have become increasingly dependent on the actions of the executives in their companies. If an executive does something which brings the company into disrepute, it is the chairman who is likely to be held responsible for the company's fall from grace. This gives chairmen good cause to take a close interest in the appointment of executives, on whom their position may at some stage depend.

In this way, the growth of the external responsibilities of chairmen has added to their internal responsibilities. This may account for some of the confusion over how far chairmen have become 'executive', regardless of the label which is attached to them. It adds up to a significant change in the role of the chairman in Britain and in other countries with similar board structures, which have been exposed to the same outside forces.

This conclusion raises the question of how far the same changes have occurred elsewhere in the world.

North America

In North America, companies command even more public attention than they do in Britain, but that has long been so. There is, therefore, less reason to expect either the role of those who head American companies or the public perception of that role to have changed to any great extent in recent years. The focus, in any case, tends to be on the Chief Executive Officer (CEO), as the personification of the company, rather than on the chairman.

Marvin Bower, in McKinsey and Co., *Effective Boardroom Management* (1971), describes the way in which American companies are organised at the top as follows:

> The most common team at the top is a team of two – the chairman and the president. Either may be the CEO, and this responsibility may shift from time to time from one of these positions to the other. The responsibilities of the two positions vary from company to company and also depend on individual capabilities. In the 100 largest US

companies, the position of CEO is held by 55 chairmen and 28 presidents. In the remaining 17, the same individual holds both titles. (p. 34)

The CEO is, therefore, usually the chairman as well, but it is as CEO that he would normally speak for the company. Two of the differences between American and British board structures are that American boards are mainly made up of outside directors and the top jobs are usually divided between a chairman and CEO, and a president and COO (Chief Operating Officer). While the way the split works in a given company will vary with the individuals concerned, as Marvin Bower says, the roles of the CEO and the COO are well established and there are generally accepted definitions of those two positions. Given that the top jobs are better defined in North America than that of the chairman in Britain, there is no obvious basis for supposing that there has been any measurable change in the way in which they are being carried out, although public scrutiny of the activities of American companies has become more intense.

What has changed in the last few years has been the balance of power within the governance structure of companies in the United States. Shareholders are becoming more vocal and outside directors more vigorous. As a result, the boards of major companies have been prepared to replace CEOs in whom they and the shareholders have lost confidence. CEOs may still personify their companies, but they are being held more effectively to account and, for the first time, the advantages of the chairman not also being the CEO are being seriously canvassed.

Japan

The key executive position in a Japanese company is normally held by the president. The emphasis in Japan, however, on co-operation and collegiality tends to limit the degree to which the president would be considered to embody the company. Jonathan Charkham, whose book *Keeping Good Company* (1994) is the authoritative source of information on comparative corporate governance, reports, 'In recent years there have been several Japanese company presidents whose public persona has seemed to indicate a stance much closer to that of an American CEO and much less close to the Japanese *primus inter pares*' (p. 90).

Nevertheless, it was the chairman of Japan Air Lines who resigned after a fatal crash, not the president. Chairmen are often former presidents and their move to the chairmanship is a step towards retirement. Boards in Japan are large bodies by British and American standards and so their proceedings must be presumed to be mainly formal. Chairmen are primarily responsible for the outward face of their companies, but where they do have power is over the appointment of the president. The president would normally be their nominee.

Apart from the exception noted by Jonathan Charkham, there is not the same focus on any one individual within the company in Japan as there is in America and Britain. There is no clear evidence, therefore, of changing roles. However, the increasingly international scope of the activities of Japanese companies may demand more of their chairmen, in the future, than it would be appropriate to ask of retired presidents.

Continental Europe

Looking finally and cursorily at Continental Europe, here there is greater precision about duties and responsibilities at the top than there is in Britain. Most job titles have clear legal responsibilities attached to them. Thus, in France, it is the Président Directeur Général (PDG) who heads the company and holds specific powers by virtue of his office. The PDG could be said to combine the jobs of chairman and CEO and, because the position has always had a legal basis, its content has not changed in recent years.

In Germany and in those countries which broadly follow the German approach to board structure, the two-tier board system ensures that direction (or supervision) and management are legally and operationally split. It is, therefore, impossible to combine the jobs of chairman and chief executive. The *Aufsichtsrat* or supervisory board meets a minimum of four times a year and the title of its chairman is the *Vorsitzender*. The *Vorstand*, i.e. the management board, is led by the managing director who is known as the *Sprecher*. He, as his title implies, is the spokesman for the management of the company and therefore normally for the company itself.

The management board is the driving force under a two-tier board structure and that board is responsible for the company's strategy as well as for the implementation of strategy. The chairman of the supervisory board stands back from the company's day-to-day management and, although responsible for its standing and reputation, would not be expected to answer for its actions in the same way as the chairman of a company board in Britain.

When a German company is in the news, there is likely to be a greater focus on personalities than in the past, for the same reasons as in Britain. This would not, however, appear to have influenced the role of either the *Sprecher* or the *Vorsitzender* to any marked extent. This is primarily because their posts are embedded in a well-defined organisational structure. In addition, the emphasis is on the *Vorstand* as a team rather than on the *Sprecher* as an individual. The two-tier board system and its variants have established a clear governance framework which has altered little in the last twenty-five years.

CONCLUSION

Caution is in order in drawing general conclusions about a role as varied and as individual as that of the chairman. There are, however, good grounds for concluding that the role of the chairman has been changing in Britain and in countries which follow the British board model. The direction of the change has been towards identifying chairmen more closely with the companies whose boards they chair and holding them increasingly accountable for the actions of their companies.

These changes have had a particular impact on the role of the chairman in those countries where the position is ill-defined and has no legal standing. As a consequence, there is confusion about what chairmen do in practice and how the post should be described. This is well illustrated by the quotation from Heidrick and Struggles' survey on page 23 above. Given the importance of the chairman's job, it would be helpful if the confusion could be reduced by greater agreement between chairmen themselves as to their duties and responsibilities.

More fundamentally, the changes in the chairman's role as described in this chapter could be expected to alter in some degree the type of person whom boards will elect as their chairmen and the way in which they will carry out their task when they are in the chair. The pressures are for chairmen to become, in Sir Walter Puckey's words, more 'executively accountable' and that will tend to change their relationship with their boards and with their chief executives if the top job is divided.

This suggests that chairmen could be chosen more for the individual leadership they can provide to their boards and companies, than for their ability to ensure that the necessary leadership comes from their boards. There is a certain tension between the role of the chairman in getting the collective best out of a board, which is a team role, and the role of the chairman as the leader of that team, which is an individual role. If there is a shift in the direction of the chairman as leader, then that would also narrow the difference between the jobs of the chairman and of the chief executive and alter the relationship between those holding these posts. It will be helpful to keep these implications of the changing role in mind, as we look in more detail at the task of the chairman.

CHAPTER 2

THE CHAIRMAN'S RESPONSIBILITY
FOR THE BOARD

If the board is not taking the company purposefully into the future,
who is? It is because of boards' failure to create tomorrow's company
out of today's that so many famous names in British Industry continue
to disappear.

Sir John Harvey-Jones

WHAT ARE BOARDS FOR?

The heart of the job of chairmen is to get the best out of their boards.
This is why their boards appointed them as chairmen and it is the one
responsibility which they cannot share or delegate. In discussing how
chairmen set about making the most of the collective abilities of their
boards, we need to consider what boards are for, who should and
should not be on them and how their effectiveness can be assessed.

The board's function is to set the company's aims and objectives
and to ensure that they are achieved. The board is the top decision-
making body in the enterprise and is the source of authority for the
managers who run its operations. The board is appointed by the
shareholders and is accountable to them for the company's progress.
It is, therefore, the vital link between the owners and the managers of
the company. Chairmen have the dual task of ensuring that their
boards direct their companies effectively and that they retain the
confidence of the shareholders; that is as true of the small family
concern as it is of the large corporation. They are responsible for
seeing that their boards hold the right balance between the interests
of the shareholders and the aims of the management, when the two
are not identical. It is, therefore, appropriate to look first at the
accountability of the board to the shareholders. This gives the board
the guidelines within which it has to work, in deciding on the purpose
of the enterprise and on how that purpose can best be achieved.

30

THE CHAIRMAN'S RESPONSIBILITY FOR THE BOARD 31

The board and the shareholders

Most businesses are started by individuals who own them and run them. They do not in their early stages have to draw the distinction between ownership and management, because both functions are vested in the same people. Some companies decide deliberately to limit their growth so as to retain the identity between ownership and management. This greatly simplifies the decision-making process, because two sets of interests do not then have to be weighed against each other. However, as soon as a company brings in outside capital, or some of its owners cease to play a part in its management, a means has to be found to keep the actions of the managers in step with the interests of the owners.

That bridge between owners and managers is the board, and it is the responsibility of chairmen to keep the board bridge in good repair. In doing so, they have continually to remind the executive directors on the board that the business does not belong to them. It is advantageous that the executives should identify themselves as fully as possible with the enterprise to which they are devoting their working lives and from which they gain their livelihood. However, it is only too easy to slip from commitment to the company's aims, which is wholly commendable, to possessiveness about what those aims should be. It is also easy to pay insufficient regard to whether those aims would receive equally enthusiastic support from the shareholders, were they to be given the chance to express their views. It is for chairmen, as the link with the shareholders, to see that their boards frame the company's purpose with the interests of the owners of the business firmly and continually in mind.

To whom do directors owe their duty?

The simple answer to this question is that it is the duty of directors to serve the interests of the shareholders. The legal answer is that they owe their duty to the company. How real is the difference between these two concepts and does the difference matter? While serving the shareholder interest is a good working definition of a director's responsibilities, to which we will return, the legal position is more complex. It is necessary to touch on some of these complexities for chairmen to be aware where they and their boards stand in relation to their duties.

First, it is clear that a company as a body corporate has a legal personality distinct from its members. A company is not, therefore, the same as its shareholders. In the leading case of *Saloman* v. *A Saloman & Co Ltd* (1897) AC22, Lord Macnaghten stated: 'The company is at law a different person altogether from the subscribers to the memorandum . . . the company is not in law the agent of the subscribers or trustee for them.'

That the company is neither the agent of the shareholders nor their trustee was made clear by the judgment of the Court of Appeal in 1908 in *The Gramophone and Typewriter Limited* v. *Stanley*. Lord Justice Buckley dismissed the argument that in practice the shareholders could be considered to be the company with the words: 'It is so familiar that it would be a waste of time to dwell upon the difference between the corporation and the aggregate of all the corporators.' He then went on to make an important statement about the relationship between the board and the shareholders:

> The directors are not servants to obey directions given by the shareholders as individuals; they are not agents appointed by and bound to serve the shareholders as their principals. They are persons who may by the regulations be entrusted with the control of the business, and if so entrusted they can be dispossessed from that control only by the statutory majority which can alter the articles. Directors are not, I think, bound to comply with the directions even of all the corporators acting as individuals.

Interestingly, the chairman of The Gramophone and Typewriter Limited (and he is referred to by the court as chairman of the company and not simply as chairman of the board) made some unwise public comments which were used by the Revenue against the company. They were, however, swept aside by Lord Justice Buckley as being 'only the expression of a layman for whose views the company is not responsible'. This is not a line of defence on which chairmen or companies should rely today!

In effect, the shareholders of a company elect its directors and entrust them with the control of the company's affairs. From there on, the directors owe their duty to the company and in following that course they may take decisions which some or all of the shareholders consider not to be in their best interests. The recourse which the shareholders have in that situation is to exercise their powers in general meeting to vote in a new board of directors whom they consider will look after their interests more faithfully.

The distinction between a company and its shareholders was clearly drawn by Lord Evershed in 1947 in a case concerning compensation for the shareholders of Short Brothers on the compulsory acquisition of their shares in 1943: 'Shareholders are not in the eye of the law, part owners of the undertaking. The undertaking is something different from the totality of the shareholdings.' The outcome of the Short Brothers' case was that the shareholders were entitled only to the market value of their shares on the day they were acquired and not to their proportion of what the company as a whole might have been said to have been worth at that time. What shareholders own are *shares*. These shares acknowledge the investment their holders have made in a company carrying on a business and confer certain rights and responsibilities on their owners. The owners are entitled to whatever dividends are declared and they have some security against the assets of the company should it be wound up. Owning shares in a company is not strictly the same as owning the business carried on by the company.

The interests of directors and shareholders

This distinction between the directors' duty to the company and to the shareholders is important, because there can be occasions when the views of the directors and the shareholders may diverge over where the company's best interests lie. The directors may regard a particular investment as serving the long-term interests of the company, even though it may be at some cost to profitability in the short term and so against the apparent short-term interests of the shareholders, or at least of some of them. This example draws attention to the fact that interests differ among shareholders. Some are more concerned with trading in a company's shares than holding them; others will differ as to the relative importance they attach to dividends and to capital appreciation. Shareholders are not a homogeneous group with a common set of interests, as chairmen soon discover.

In the long-term versus short-term argument over the level of investment, the directors may well have a strong case in the interests of the company for overriding the immediate apparent interests of the shareholders or, if you like, going counter to the decision which the majority of shareholders might have made in a vote on the matter. The directors would argue that the shareholders would benefit in the longer run from an improvement in the earning power and capital value of the business as a result of the investment. In doing so, the directors will be taking account of the future needs of present shareholders.

When it is a question of making an acquisition, shareholders in public companies do have the opportunity to express their views if the acquisition is of a certain size. A more contentious issue would be one which involved the choice between re-investing in the business, perhaps taking it in a new direction, and returning cash to the shareholders through higher dividends. In the past there was a taxation argument in Britain for re-investment, because capital appreciation was taxed at a lower rate than income. This meant that the interests of the company and those of the shareholders could be held to coincide in support of a policy of corporate growth rather than of higher dividends to shareholders.

That argument is less relevant now in countries such as Britain, where income and capital are taxed more evenly. It would be understandable for directors to see the continued growth and development of the business as a self-evident objective and one which commended itself to them. From their perspective it would mean being involved with an expanding enterprise and it could also be argued to be in the interests of the company, on the basis that bigger was likely on balance to be better. It is, however, for the chairman and the board to test whether bigger is likely to be better from the shareholders' viewpoint and to weigh the case for investing shareholders' funds on their behalf against allowing them to invest their proportion of those funds for themselves.

Directors' duties

Chairmen need to be aware that the law distinguishes between the duties of directors to the company and their responsibilities to their shareholders. To the layman, the difference would appear to be one of timing. In the long run it is difficult to see how the interests of the company could be different from the interests of those who have invested in it; in the short run those interests can diverge. The company, however, is a continuing entity, while those holding shares in it will come and go. The board has a duty to ensure the continuity of the company, exceptional circumstances aside, but not necessarily in its existing form. In furtherance of that duty, it can take actions which will primarily benefit the company in the future and so advantage tomorrow's shareholders rather than today's. How far tomorrow's shareholders are the same as today's is a matter for the shareholders themselves.

In practice, this discussion of the duties of directors brings us back to the starting-point. The safest course for directors is to keep the interests of the shareholders, who appointed them and who can dismiss them, always in mind. Geoffrey Mills, in *Controlling Companies*, quotes with approval a statement by the American Bar Association: 'The fundamental responsibility of the individual corporate director is to represent the interests of the shareholders as a group, as the owners of the enterprise, in directing the business and affairs of the corporation within the law' (p. 156). Although based on the legal position of directors in the United States, it is good advice and if followed would be a sound defence against shareholders' suits. It is worth noting that representing the interests of the shareholders is referred to as the *fundamental* responsibility of directors and not their *sole* responsibility. I regard the board as being accountable to the share-holders, but responsible to a wider constituency, an issue which will be discussed in a later chapter. Accountability is a more limited concept than responsibility and describes the way in which the board is held to account for its stewardship by the shareholders in general meeting.

The definition of purpose

The board represents the interests of the shareholders by setting the company's aims and by monitoring their achievement. It is, therefore, the function of the board to define the purpose of the company. The company's purpose can be defined in terms of the products or services it will offer, the markets it will enter, the financial targets it will meet or some combination of all three.

One of the best-known statements of corporate purpose is that of IBM, which is expressed in quite different terms because it is based on that corporation's three beliefs. These are as follows: the belief in respect for the individual; the belief in giving the best customer service of any company in the world; and the belief that an organisation should pursue all tasks with the idea that they can be accomplished in a superior fashion. These beliefs are set out in the book on the business which Thomas Watson wrote in 1963.

However a company's purpose is expressed, it is the job of the board to see that the aims of the enterprise are clear, that they are kept up to date and that they are backed by the commitment of those who are charged with carrying them out. It is for the board to provide the company with a sense of vision, as well as a sense of direction. If the company is to make the most of its opportunities, then the board has to be the source of inspiration for the attainment of the goals that it sets. The board is also responsible for the way in which a company achieves its goals and, therefore, for the kind of enterprise it is and aims to become.

The board as the driving force

Kenneth Dayton summed up the function of the board, as I see it, forcefully and well in an article he wrote in the *Harvard Business Review* (January–February 1984), about his own company Dayton Hudson. This is how he put it:

> For this reason we state clearly in the board's position description that it is the board's function as representatives of the shareholders to be the primary force pressing the corporation to the realization of its opportunities and the fulfilment of its obligations to its shareholders, customers, employees and the communities in which it operates.

This definition links the board's responsibilities to the shareholders, which have already been discussed, with its duty to be the driving force within the company. This is a powerful statement of purpose for chairmen to have in mind. In too many companies the board is not the primary force and is relegated to a monitoring – or even worse, a rubber-stamping – role.

As an example of the opposite to the Dayton Hudson approach I have included, in Appendix 2, a sceptical view of the board composed by a fellow confectionery manufacturer in France in the 1930s. I owe this insight to the International Institute for Management Development (IMD) Lausanne, which runs a highly regarded programme for members of boards and is carrying out original and important research into the way in which boards work.

While it is for the board as a whole to recognise its responsibility to lead and inspire the company, it is for the chairman to keep this primary aim before the board.

Strategies, plans and policies

If the board is to be the primary force in ensuring that the company makes the most of its opportunities, it has to determine not only the company's goals but also the manner of their achievement. The board is, therefore, responsible for the strategy of the business and for agreeing the operating plans and targets required to turn the strategy into action. It does this in conjunction with the management who have the responsibility for achieving the results. The final strategy and action plans may well move between the board and the management more than once, so that the outcome is a board/management dialogue rather than the board passing a set of instructions on to those who have to execute them. In this way both board and management commit themselves to a mutually agreed strategy.

It is up to chairmen to concentrate the attention of their boards on the part which they alone can play in forming strategy, so preventing board members becoming involved in the task of management rather than that of direction. The board is responsible for the company's purpose and for satisfying itself that the courses of action proposed by the management are the best on offer. Anything that boards can delegate to the management they should, and it is for chairmen to see that they do.

People

The board's aims are achieved by people; consequently, another side of the board's function as the driving force is for it to be certain that the right executives are in the appropriate driving seats. The key appointment is that of the chief executive, or managing director, and the importance of the board's decision as to who should be in executive charge of the business needs no emphasising. It is the responsibility of boards to appoint their chief executives and to ensure that they continue to measure up to the post, the demands of which will be continually changing, especially in a fast-growing company.

Appointing and, if necessary, replacing the chief executive are not only crucial board functions, but they are extremely demanding and difficult ones. Chairmen, therefore, have a particular responsibility for seeing that every possible step is taken to make the best appointment in the first place and that thereafter the board formally reviews the progress of their chief executives and lets them know regularly how their performance is rated. If they do not meet the board's standards, the board then has to face up to replacing them. Chairmen – those who are not chief executives as well – have to take the lead in this review process.

Summary of board functions

I would summarise the main functions of the board as follows:

- to define the company's purpose;
- to agree the strategies and plans for achieving that purpose;
- to establish the company's policies;
- to appoint the chief executive;
- to review the performance of the chief executive and the executive team;
- in all this to be the driving force in the company.

The board carries out these functions in its role as the final point of decision within the business. In particular, the board allocates the company's resources of people and of cash through its decisions on top appointments and on the direction of investment. The task of chairmen is to keep their boards focused on those functions which they alone can perform. In terms of the board's accountability to the shareholders, the need is to ensure that the board sees its decisions through the eyes of the shareholders. It is the board which has to hold the balance between the immediate and the longer-term interests of the company in the ultimate interests of the shareholders.

BOARD REVIEW

There is, however, one further duty which falls to boards and that is to review how far and how well they have carried out the functions just discussed. How should a board set about reviewing its own work? Boards have just as much need to assess their performance as individuals, and the object in both cases is the same: it is to learn from the past in order to be able to do better in the future. It is up to chairmen to decide how to go about such a collective assessment. It probably means meeting away from the office in order to gain greater detachment and to be able to give undivided attention to the question of how well the board is doing its job.

One of the most valuable resources available to the company is the time of its board, so the first set of questions which need to be asked relate to the way in which the board has used its time. Did it concentrate on those issues which it is uniquely capable of resolving? Peter Drucker once wrote that priorities were easy, but that it was posteriorities – what jobs *not* to tackle – which were tough. Priorities are not that easy, but I fully accept that posteriorities are even more difficult. The board needs to appraise its choice of priorities and posteriorities. One aspect of the use of time is whether the board believes that it spends enough time overall in the fulfilment of its responsibilities.

Other points for the board to consider relate to the decisions it has taken. Looking back, could either the decisions themselves or the process by which they were arrived at have been improved? What was there to be learnt for the future about the decisions that the board did make?

Then there is a range of questions relating to the way in which the board works as a team. These cover the relationships between board members and the degree of openness with which sensitive issues can be discussed.

Chairmen who want a more precise set of questions against which to test the effectiveness of their boards could not do better than to turn to the first of Hugh Parker's *Letters to a New Chairman* (1990, p. 12). In that letter he lists six questions which chairmen need to ask of themselves and of their boards. I have included Hugh Parker's checklist as Appendix 3, because it forms the best basis I have yet come across for a board to analyse whether it has its priorities right.

Assessment methods

A more formal approach to self-assessment is described in a report, published in 1994 by the National Association of Corporate Directors of the United States, entitled *Performance Evaluation of Chief Executive Officers, Boards and Directors*. It sets out a structured method for boards and board committees to assess how well they are discharging their responsibilities, which breaks down the evaluation of board performance into three segments: the performance of the board as a whole, the performance of the board leadership – board and committee chairmen – and the performance of the individual directors.

What is difficult to capture with an evaluation system of this kind, as the report recognises, is the way in which board members interact with each other, on which the effectiveness of the board depends. A major benefit, however, is that it requires the board to agree, in the first place, on the nature of their duties and responsibilities.

As an alternative to boards reviewing their own performance, an external assessor can be used. The chairman of Southern New England Telephone, A. W. van Sinderen, describes, in an interesting article, how his board brought in an outside consultant to conduct an independent evaluation of its effectiveness. The evaluation proved to be of considerable benefit to board members and sorted out some problems of whose existence the board was previously unaware. What the consultant, an academic, brought to the review process was experience in working with boards and objectivity.

The company's results in the market-place are one objective measure of the board's success in directing the business. But only the board can judge whether it set the company's sights high enough, especially in relation to its competitors. The outside world looks at a company's results year by year, but the board is concerned with continuity. Thus the board, in determining how well it has fulfilled its responsibilities, will need to assess how far it has maintained the momentum of the business and how well it has balanced the needs of the future against the needs of the present. These are judgements which the board alone can make in reviewing its own record; it is the chairman's job to see that the board carries out such a review and that it puts the lessons learnt from it into practice.

Review of individual board members

In addition to appraising the performance of the board as a whole, chairmen can gain a great deal from appraisal discussions with directors individually. Henry Wendt, chairman of SmithKline Beecham, has an annual appraisal interview with each of his outside directors. Their discussion covers such matters as attendance, grasp of key issues and especially level and quality of participation in board deliberations. Henry Wendt makes the point that if an outside director does not participate effectively in discussions at the board, this diminishes the value of the board as a whole. SmithKline Beecham gives its outside directors specific assignments in relation to one of the company's business sectors and the way they discharge that responsibility adds a further dimension to the appraisal.

Such discussions assist outside directors to make a better contribution to the work of the board and they also have their part to play in decisions about changes in board membership. Although appraisals at SmithKline Beecham are confined to the outside directors, they could be at least as useful to executive directors, given that such directors have to resolve the tensions inherent in their dual roles as executives and as directors. They will be appraised by their chief executive in respect of their management task and it would seem logical for them also to be appraised by their chairman in regard to their contribution as a board director.

From a chairman's point of view, as I know from my own experience, any appraisal discussion with individual directors rapidly changes direction and becomes an appraisal of the chairman. Directors may well feel that the limitations on their ability to participate effectively in the board's work are in the hands of the chairman. They may consider that the lack of relevant, timely information, or the way in which debates are handled and decisions made, make it difficult for them to contribute as well as they might.

Chairmen need to know what their directors feel is holding them back and what changes in board procedures, or in their chairmanship, would release their energies more effectively. Chairmen cannot improve their contribution to the working of their boards without this kind of honest and constructive feedback. Appraisal interviews with individual directors are an excellent way for chairmen to appraise themselves.

CHAPTER 3

BOARD MEMBERSHIP

The job of corporate governance today is too great for any chairman to do alone. That's why you need a board. The primary job of the chairman is to run the board.

Sir John Harvey-Jones

WHY HAVE A BOARD?

The virtual absence of any reference to boards in Britain's Companies Acts raises the question whether it is necessary to have a board at all. Could not the board's functions be carried out by one or two individuals? Legally and operationally they could be, but the support worldwide for boards of a kind at the head of all manner of public and private bodies is a measure of the arguments in their favour. In the first place there are obvious disadvantages, stemming from concentration of power, lack of checks and balances, and problems over succession, in putting all authority into individual hands.

The essential advantage of the board approach was well expressed by the Roman dramatist Plautus in around 200 BC, when he wrote – '*Nemo solus satis sapit*'. In English less polished than the Latin, this means that no one on their own is wise enough. The board provides a means of bringing a variety of minds and of viewpoints, backed by a variety of experience, to bear on the issues which confront a company. The board is a deliberative body and at its meetings ideas are formed and turned into plans of action, through debate. It provides those who have the executive responsibility for running a company with an informed sounding-board with which they can usefully interact.

Almost every proposition which comes before a board can, in my experience, be improved upon, if it is worked through with a group of people from different backgrounds who share a common aim. I have no doubt about the advantages of the board approach, but, to realise them, chairmen themselves must believe in the value of boards and be determined to make the most of the resource which their boards represent. They need also to have properly constituted boards with the right mix of people on them.

WHO SHOULD BE ON THE BOARD?

Board size

The first decision in relation to the make-up of a board is what its overall size should be. The balance is between a body which is small enough for there to be true debate and discussion between members and large enough to bring in the range of knowledge and experience which chairmen and their boards feel that they need. Sir Walter Puckey writes that in his experience

> the board's most effective size is between six and eight excluding the chairman and the secretary, who may or may not be a director. Too many board meetings display verbosity among a few and almost complete silence among the rest. (Puckey 1969, p. 85)

Martin Lipton and Jay W. Lorsch, who have contributed so constructively to the debate on corporate governance in the United States and internationally, argue persuasively for a reduction in the size of American boards. In their 'Modest Proposal for Improved Corporate Governance', they recommend that boards should be limited to a maximum of ten directors. Indeed, they would favour boards of eight or nine. They reason that smaller boards will encourage directors to get to know each other well, to have more effective discussions with all directors contributing, and to reach a true consensus from their deliberations.

Other authorities edge the figure up: Harold Koontz, in *The Board of Directors and Effective Management*, for example, suggests that it is sensible 'to limit a board to thirteen members in order to obtain the free discussion and deliberative interplay which board decisions require'. At the upper end, Professor Northcote Parkinson's researches have demonstrated conclusively that what he refers to as the 'coefficient of inefficiency' is reached when the members of a body number between nineteen and twenty-two; at that point an inner cabinet is established, or establishes itself, to take over the functions of the original board or committee.

Common sense suggests that a board should be no larger than it needs to be to meet Harold Koontz's requirements of free discussion and deliberative interplay. Owner/managers moving to a board structure will want to start with as small a board as possible, since the choice of the founding board members is so critical. For companies which market their goods and services internationally, I would pitch my range above Sir Walter Puckey's and would suggest around nine to twelve members, excluding the secretary. Apart from anything else, with the pressure of travel and other commitments, boards will not all that often be at their full strength. Those numbers still allow for effective debate and it is the job of chairmen to restrain the verbosity of the few and to encourage the participation of the majority.

Insiders and outsiders

Chairmen are looking for a balance of experience and points of view on their boards, within whatever totals are appropriate to the size of their companies. On unitary boards, the main balance is between executive directors and outside or non-executive directors. I prefer the term 'outside director', which is used in North America, to the generally accepted British description of such directors, as 'non-executive'. I consider that it reflects more accurately the position of these directors as members of the board team. They lack the executive directors' inside knowledge of the workings of the business, but bring outside experience and independence of judgement to the work of the board. Building an effective unitary board team starts with achieving the right mix of outsiders and insiders.

Independence

The term 'independent director' is sometimes used as if it were synonymous with 'outside director'. Not all outside directors, however, are independent. An outside director who is from the company's legal advisers or merchant bankers is not as independent as a director who has no business connections with the company. Equally, executive directors, who retire from the company and remain on the board, become outside directors, but they cannot be classed as independent because of the closeness of their links with the executive management of the company.

This distinction does not mean that board members who have a business relationship with a company, but are not executives, cannot contribute fully and effectively to its board – they can and do. It is, however, a different contribution from that made by directors who do not owe their livelihood to the company. The special attributes which these directors bring to the working of a unitary board are objectivity and independence of judgement.

There was no way of estimating the proportion of outside directors who had some form of business link with their companies, until a survey in 1985 by the Bank of England of the board structure of the 1,000 largest industrial companies. The survey showed that a surprisingly high proportion of outside directors were not strictly independent. Three in five of the responding companies had appointed professional advisers or former executives as outside directors and such directors accounted for nearly one in two of the outside directors included in the survey. A follow-up survey in 1987 revealed that there had been a sharp drop in the proportion of non-independent, outside directors. At least 75 per cent of the outside directors covered were found to have had no present or previous professional relationship with their company, nor had they served as an executive.

The issue of the degree of independence of directors was further highlighted by the report of the Committee on the Financial Aspects of Corporate Governance in 1992. The Committee defined independent directors as those who, apart from their directors' fees and shareholdings, were independent of management and free from any business or other relationship which could materially interfere with the exercise of their independent judgement. The report said that it was for boards to decide in the first instance which of their members met this test of independence, a judgement which could then be confirmed by the shareholders, provided that companies made a full disclosure of the interests of their directors in their annual reports. The Bank of England had also drawn attention to the need for a greater degree of disclosure of directors' interests in its *Bank Bulletin* commentary on the 1987 survey results.

The distinction between outside directors and independent outside directors is underlined in the Committee's proposals on audit committees. The Committee recommended that audit committees should be formally constituted as sub-committees of the main board, to whom they are answerable and to whom they should report regularly. They should have a minimum of three members, all of whom should be outside directors, with a majority being independent as defined in the previous paragraph.

The Committee's recommendation that only outside directors should serve on the audit committee led to the misunderstanding that this implied a lack of trust in executive directors, as though trust was in finite supply and could only be vested in the outside directors at the expense of executive board members. This interpretation of the Committee's proposals was wrong on two counts. First, the audit committee reports to the board and so all board members remain equally responsible for the integrity of the company's financial statements. Second, the basis of differentiation between executive and independent outside directors is simply that they are less likely to be affected by conflicts of interest. The interests of the company and those of the executives may at times diverge, for example over such issues as takeovers, management buy-outs, boardroom succession or directors' pay. Independent outside directors, whose interests are less directly affected, are best placed to help the board to resolve such issues.

The role of the outside director

The argument for having a proportion of outside directors on the board is that the board needs to be able to stand back from the management of the business, because it is responsible for directing it and not for running it from day to day. Executive directors, therefore, have to change hats when they sit as board members. They are no longer in charge of their particular side of the business, they are concerned with the interests of the company as a whole. This is inevitably a difficult switch to make, particularly when the board is discussing issues which directly affect the executive director's field of responsibility. Executive directors are helped, in drawing the essential distinction between their role as executives and their role as directors, by having outside board members as colleagues who have no such potential conflicts of interest. The advantages of having outside directors on a board can be seen clearly in respect of two of the board's functions.

Appraisal

First, the board is responsible for setting the aims of the company and for seeing that those aims are achieved. The board, therefore, has the task of assessing the company's performance and taking whatever action is necessary to maintain that performance at the level it has set. This puts the wholly executive board in the position of invigilating itself. Lord Caldecote, the former chairman of The Delta Group, is quoted by Robert Tricker in the opening sentence of *Corporate Governance* as saying, 'The trouble with British companies is that the directors mark their own examination papers.' At least outside directors are external examiners and able to mark the company's progress papers with a certain objectivity.

If self-invigilation is a difficult enough task without outside help, then sitting in judgement on your boss is even more difficult. Another of the board's primary functions is to appraise, and if found wanting to replace, the chief executive. But the executive directors as managers report to their chief executives and are appraised by them. It is unrealistic to expect them as directors to reverse the process, still less to tell their chief executives that they think they should make way for someone else. Yet serious appraisal and counselling as to the way they are doing their job are essential to chief executives if they are to improve their performance.

Frank advice of this kind can best be provided by directors who are not beholden to chief executives for their jobs. Arguably, boards in Britain have not on the whole carried out this function of setting and demanding high standards of executive performance as well as they should have done. It is hard to see how they could where there was not an effective, independent presence on the board.

I have selected the board's appraisal functions as examples of essential tasks which will be better carried out if there are outside directors on the board. The argument for having an outside element on the board, however, is much more positive than the fact that there are certain vital board functions which it is difficult for executive directors to carry out to the full on their own. Jonathan Charkham sets out the case for independent directors admirably and authoritatively in his book *Effective Boards: The independent element and the role of the non-executive director*, published in 1986.

Positive participation

If I had to pick out one field in which I believe outside directors have a particularly useful role to play in contributing to the successful progress of an enterprise, it would be in the formulation of strategy. It is a misunderstanding to suppose that outside directors cannot contribute to a company's strategy because they do not have sufficient depth of knowledge of the business. It is precisely because they are not immersed in the detail of the company's activities that they are free to ask questions, the answers to which the executive directors may too readily take for granted.

Cadbury Schweppes made a major strategic change of direction in 1986 when the company sold two of its business streams, foods and household products, in order to concentrate its efforts behind the international development of its confectionery and soft drink businesses. That policy change came about through the board asking what results would stem from putting all the company's resources behind its two main branded businesses. The outside directors were in the best position to ask that kind of vital, but uncomfortable, question which only the executive team could answer. Thus, outside directors can help to shape strategy, not through knowing the business better than management, but through asking the right questions. The final decisions on strategy are then taken by the board collectively, drawing on the contributions of executive and outside directors alike.

I believe that outside directors add vitality to a board. They balance the knowledge of the business of insiders with the supportive but critical objectivity of outsiders. They broaden the board's outlook and stand ready to question what those of us who have worked in one business all our lives may well take for granted. The participation of outside directors breathes fresh life into the board's discussions and brings out the best in the executive directors. A leaven of outsiders of the right kind improves the effectiveness of the board as a whole.

Angus Murray is quoted by Geoffrey Mills as defining what chairmen are looking for from their outside directors:

> A good non-executive director needs to have intellect, integrity and courage. Of these qualities, courage is the most important, for without it the other two characteristics are useless. (Mills 1988, p. 94)

As to what the balance between insiders and outsiders should be, that is a matter for individual chairmen and their boards to decide. The most favoured balance in Britain today is probably around one-third outside directors and two-thirds executive directors, with the proportion of outside directors gradually rising. In the United States, the majority of board members would be outsiders. The lower limit on the number of outside directors is that there should be enough of them for their views to carry weight in board discussions and for them to be able to work together within the board, as well as with their executive colleagues. This question of the numbers of outside and executive directors on a board leads on to the issue of how board members should be chosen.

PRO NED

At this point I should declare my interest in the appointment of outside directors, which derives from my chairmanship of PRO NED. PRO NED was established in 1982 under the sponsorship of a group of institutions representative of industry and finance, led by the Bank of England. It exists to promote recognition of the crucial contribution which outside directors of the right calibre can make to company boards, and to help companies find appropriate candidates for such appointments. I became involved in PRO NED's work because I firmly believe that the appointment of properly selected outside directors improves board effectiveness. PRO NED has now moved, from being sponsored by a group of interested institutions, to being owned by those who run it in partnership with Egon Zehnder International. This partnership provides the international breadth of resource which is required to meet the board needs of large public companies today. Virtually all such companies recognise the contribution which capable outside directors make to boards. There is still some way to go, however, in persuading smaller and medium-sized companies of the advantages of having carefully chosen outsiders on their boards.

The appointment of directors

It is for chairmen to take the lead in determining how large their boards should be and how they should be constituted. The boards they inherit on their appointment may not be capable of giving their companies the leadership that they believe they should. If so, they will want to change the composition of their boards, either in one move or over a period, and those who appointed them chairmen should have done so in the knowledge of their views on the kind of board which they believed their company needed. Whether chairmen have to alter the shape of their boards when they are appointed or not, they will need to do so over time as the nature of the challenges facing the company alters. A deliberate policy of renewal is necessary in any case, if a board is not to become ossified and lose its vital spark.

Board tenure

What this adds up to is that all board members should have agreed terms of appointment. This goes, in my view, for governing bodies of any kind; the more voluntary and less structured they are, the more important it is that their officers should come up regularly for review. To return to boards, however, if directors are appointed, say, for a three-year term, then, when their term is drawing to an end, an opportunity is created for chairmen and the directors concerned to meet to discuss the position. Such an end-of-term review is no substitute for the annual appraisals of outside directors referred to in the previous chapter. It does, however, give outside directors the opportunity to discuss how well the board is working from their viewpoint, and enables chairmen to go over with outside directors the individual contributions they are making to the working of the board.

In the light of these discussions, there can be mutual agreement on whether a further three-year appointment makes sense to both sides. A fixed term of appointment avoids the awkwardness of having to set up a similar review meeting for no apparent reason, at least as far as the director is concerned. Quite apart from enabling re-appointment as a board member to be a positive decision, review meetings give both the chairman and the directors the chance to improve the way they do their jobs. The principle of an agreed term of office should apply to chairmen along with the other members of the board.

In referring to a three-year term, I am not suggesting that directors should serve on a board for only three years. This clearly could not apply to executive directors and would make little sense for outside directors, since much of their first term would be taken up with becoming acquainted with the company and the people in it. Nevertheless, some appointments do not work out as expected on one side or the other, and in those cases an outside director might only serve one term.

At the other end of the scale, I believe that there is merit in not remaining as an outside director on one board for life, so to speak. I have myself felt that I have contributed all that I could to a particular board and yet that I was still able to bring a fresh outlook to the board of another company. In retiring from the first board, I gave its chairman the opportunity to bring on someone in my place with a new set of ideas and interests. Given that independence of judgement is the special quality which outside directors bring to the board, there is much to be said for not staying on a board so long as to become absorbed into the company, thus losing something of your independent edge.

Nomination process

This emphasis on independence highlights the importance of the process by which nominations for the board come forward. A survey published by KPMG Peat Marwick in May 1994 showed that just over half the responding companies' outside board candidates were selected personally by the chairman. A fundamental disadvantage of this approach is that directors who owe, or who feel they owe, their position on a board to the choice of the chairman, will have their independence undermined to that extent from the outset. In the past, it was accepted that chairmen should have a power of patronage, on the basis that chairmen needed to choose board members who would work well with them and well with each other. Patronage is a pleasurable form of power and it requires strength of mind for chairmen to forgo it voluntarily, but it is incompatible with the standards of professionalism and effectiveness demanded of boards today.

It is in this context that the Committee on the Financial Aspects of Corporate Governance recommended that outside directors should be selected with the same impartiality and care as senior executives and that their appointment should be made a matter for the board as a whole, through a formal selection process. The Committee went on to say that it regarded it as good practice for nomination committees to carry out the selection process and to make proposals to the board.

Outside directors selected in this way are in a position to exercise their independence of judgement and will know that their nomination has the backing of the board as a whole and not solely that of the chairman or the chief executive. Two other consequences flow from adopting a formal process for the appointment of outside directors. The first is that the more all board members are involved in the selection process and the more professionally it is carried out, the greater the mutual respect between board members. Executive directors will have reached the board in manifest competition with their colleagues and they rightly expect their fellow directors to have been similarly chosen, openly and on merit. A second consequence is that chairmen can then explain convincingly how their outside directors came to find a place on their boards in answer to questions from shareholders and employees.

Board balance

In considering how their boards should be made up, chairmen are looking for balance, not only between inside knowledge and outside experience, but balance in terms of personalities, skills and age. The effectiveness of a board is a reflection of how well its members work together collectively as a team. What counts is not simply the presence of outside directors, nor how many there are in relation to the number of executive directors. What counts is whether the outside directors work effectively together and whether they work effectively with the executive directors. Chairmen consider potential board members in terms of the contribution which they could make to the working of the board as a collective whole.

As a consequence, what will qualify executives to become board members are the qualities they can bring to the board's activities. Clearly their function in the company is relevant, but the argument for executives joining the board should not be on the grounds that they hold key posts. Rather, the grounds should be that only someone of board calibre should be the holder of such a key post. It is the wider attributes which executives might bring to boards, rather than their management responsibilities, which make them board candidates.

It is unfortunate that in Britain so much standing should be attached to board membership; the position in the United States, where it is the executive office that counts, is a healthier one. As a result of this concern with status, there is always pressure to appoint executives as directors for reasons other than the qualities that they can bring to the collective deliberations of the board. Chairmen have to be resolute in agreeing to the appointment of executives to the board solely on their individual merits as potential directors.

Outside candidates

With outside appointments, chairmen are searching for directors with the ability to use their experience in other fields to look critically at the company's activities and to test the assumptions which insiders may accept without question. For example, as insiders, we are unlikely to challenge the standards of achievement to which we should be working, the quality of the people with whom we work and so on, and it is disturbing to have such accepted features of our business lives questioned.

Another attribute, therefore, which is required of effective outside directors, is that they should be able to ask uncomfortable questions in a constructive way – a point that has already been made in relation to formulating strategy. They need to be in sympathy with the company and its aims and critical with a view to improving the company's performance, not disparaging it. The choice of an individual outsider, as with an insider, will turn on what they can add to the board team. This is very different from saying that chairmen are looking for members who will 'fit'. If a board becomes like a club and directors are appointed for their clubability, it will not do its duty by the shareholders. The words 'board team' are used precisely because different types of talent are required to make up a team. It is the blend of individual differences and the ability to work together that distinguish a winning team.

It follows from the need for balance that chairmen want to spread their nets as widely as possible in making up their boards. Executive candidates will be well known to the existing board members, who will have a basis for judging the kind of contribution they could make. Executive appointees will not all come from the same mould and, in companies with international operations, may include nationals of other countries. Thus chairmen can arrive at a degree of balance on their boards through the executive directors appointed to them.

Filling vacancies

The appointment of outside directors, however, is a more risky process as the candidates are most unlikely to be known to all board members, who are even less likely to have had any experience of working with them. What will be important to chairmen is that they should have as wide a choice of suitable people as possible. This brings us back to the importance of the nomination process. By using an outside agency, whether it be PRO NED or an executive search firm, chairmen and their boards will be able to exercise choice. In this way they can ensure that they put forward the best board candidates they can find, rather than the first ones to obtain sufficient support for their nomination to go ahead.

The first stage in filling a board vacancy is to establish what kind of skills, experience and background would most usefully complement those of the existing board members. The search should start with the task, not as it so often does – especially when the public sector is involved – with names. In the past, chairmen mainly relied for nominations on people known to themselves, or on names put forward by other board members or the company's professional advisers. The issue of patronage apart, appointment through personal recommendation has a number of obvious drawbacks. It is based on choosing individuals, rather than on identifying gaps in the make-up of the board team and then searching for people who could fill them. Above all, it can draw only from the limited pool of names known to those involved. At its worst, the word-of-mouth approach was used to repay favours. At its best, it still led to the appointment of directors largely from the same background as that of the existing board members. While outside directors who are executives of other companies may well form the basis of the outside element of a board, the case for appointing some directors who are less likely to share the same mindset as the executive directors, becomes stronger as boards are increasingly held to account for their external responsibilities.

An important advantage of using an outside agency to find potential board candidates is that this injects a degree of competition into the selection process. Instead of appointing an acceptable candidate, boards are able to appoint the best of those whose names are put forward. This raises board standards and also gives confidence to those appointed through a formal selection process. In particular, women board candidates who know that they have been selected in competition with men, can take their place on a board with more assurance as a result.

This question of board balance might seem to be mainly an issue for large public companies, but this is not so. Owner/managers can probably achieve all the balance they want, or are likely to accept, from their professional advisers. But once the ownership is divided among a number of shareholding directors in a private company, then an outside element on the board can be an essential counterweight to the views of the owners, who may in any case not always see eye to eye. The same is true for family companies. If a board is dominated by owners and managers, who are also related, then it will be particularly important to find the right kind of outside directors. They will have to be both independent and forceful enough to keep the board's duty to the company continually before it.

WHO SHOULD NOT BE ON BOARDS?

We have already ruled out as candidates for the board executive directors whose claims are based on length of service or managerial competence. The sole criterion is directorial capacity, and appointments to the board are calls to service, not rewards for loyalty.

Friends of the chairman

Friends of the chairman are another category of unsuitable candidates, although they should not be excluded solely because they happen to know the chairman or other board members, if they are otherwise well qualified. It is essential to avoid what the Americans refer to as the 'buddy' system of appointments. The reasons are straightforward and have already been discussed. They relate to the vital attribute of outside directors, which is their independence of judgement. The same issue of independence arises regarding another class of people who, in my view, have no place on a unitary board – and they are representative directors.

Representative directors

The issue of representative directors on boards became a matter of debate in Britain with the publication of the Bullock Report in 1977. The Report was not primarily concerned with running companies more efficiently, but with changing the balance of power within them. Its basic proposal was that employee representatives should be appointed to the boards of British companies. There were numerous weaknesses in the Report's proposals, and there were two fundamental flaws in the reasoning which lay behind them, which explain why directors representing an interest cannot be members of a unitary board.

The heart of the matter is that all directors of a unitary board have an equal legal responsibility for the affairs of the company they direct and they owe it an equal duty. It is not possible to square the idea of directors representing a particular interest with the concept of a unitary board, on which all the directors have the same rights and responsibilities.

If employee directors had been appointed to unitary boards as Bullock recommended, then either the directors would have ceased to be employee directors, or their boards would have ceased to be unitary, because the two concepts are incompatible. If employee directors accept the same responsibilities as their fellow directors, they are no longer employee directors, but the board has retained its unitary nature. If, however, they remain employee directors then the board is no longer unitary. This is the main reason why any form of direct representation of special interests is unworkable on the British model of the board.

The second flaw is that Bullock appeared to believe that directors were on the board solely as representatives of the shareholders' interests in a narrow sense. The Report says:

> The extension of industrial democracy . . . can only be achieved in our view if there is direct representation of employees on company boards in just the same way as there is direct representation of shareholders on boards at present. (Cmd 6706, p. 71)

But the legal position, as we saw in the previous chapter, is that directors owe their duty to the company; they are not simply representatives of the shareholders appointed to promote the latter's interests. If that interpretation is right, then the only way in which employee interests (or the interests of shareholders) could be represented on the board in the way Bullock supposed, would be by changing the law. The law would have to be altered to the effect that directors no longer owed an overriding duty to the company.

An inevitable reaction to the Bullock proposals was that other interests advanced their claims to board representation, most notably consumer groups who saw shareholders and employees as likely to put the interests of producers before those of consumers. The argument did not, of course, stop with consumers. However, the appointment of directors representing any specific interest would undermine the unitary nature of the board. It would then have to become a forum for resolving the differences between the interest groups represented on it – not a cheering prospect for chairmen.

What is clear is that a representational board as postulated by Bullock could not be the driving force in the company. This is not to say that the way in which interests should be represented in society and how the balance of power between them should be struck are not issues of great importance, but they need to be considered separately from how the members of an efficient board should be chosen.

To the extent that the concern behind the Bullock proposals was that directors came from too narrow a social grouping, then the outside element on a board presents opportunities for widening the backgrounds from which directors are drawn. In the United States, with their predominantly outside boards, there have been deliberate moves to ensure that, for example, more women directors and black directors were appointed to boards. What is in the interest neither of the boards nor of the individuals concerned, is that this entirely understandable objective should be allowed to drift into 'tokenism', that is to say, appointing someone not for who they are, but for what they might be thought to represent.

The 3i experience

The 3i organisation in Britain provides an excellent example of how a venture capital institution with a stake in a number of companies can strengthen the boards of those companies, without requiring representation on them. The group has established a bank of experienced directors, who are available to be nominated to company boards. Its booklet, *The Role and Contribution of an Independent Director,* sets out the way in which companies, mainly those in which 3i has an investment, can draw on this resource. It opens with the statement: 'The independent director nominated by 3i has the same responsibilities and obligations to the company as the other directors.' There is no question of directors appointed through the good offices of 3i representing their interest. They are nominated, but they are independent, and they are brought into the company with the straightforward aim of strengthening its board.

CONCLUSIONS ON BOARD MEMBERSHIP

Who is on the board will determine its effectiveness and it is the duty of chairmen to see that their boards are made up of the best people available. It is for chairmen to ensure that there is an established formal process for bringing nominations forward to the board. It is for the board as a whole to agree these nominations and it is for the shareholders in general meeting to confirm them.

At Cadbury Schweppes, we had a chairman's committee, which was made up of the outside directors with myself as chairman. That committee discussed all prospective board changes, so that internal or external board candidates were only approached with its support. When the chairman's committee was ready to put a name to the board, I talked the proposal over with the executive directors individually and in this way had a clear feel for the way in which the board would view the nomination when it came formally before them.

Board appointments are a sensitive issue for chairmen, because of the need to weigh up the contribution which potential directors could make as individuals and as members of the board team. Chairmen need board members who will work together, but they also need directors who will speak their minds, who are prepared to challenge the majority view and to challenge the chairman's views when necessary.

No company should settle for anything less than a board which can provide it with a driving force. If the board is not of that measure, the responsibility is the chairman's. As so often, however, responsibilities run in both directions. It is for chairmen to see that their boards are competent and for boards to see that they have competent chairmen.

CHAPTER 4

THE CHAIRMAN AND BOARD STRUCTURE

Whenever an institution malfunctions as consistently as boards of directors have in nearly every major fiasco of the last 40 or 50 years it is futile to blame men. It is the institution that malfunctions.

Peter Drucker

BOARDS UNDER ATTACK

The quotation with which this chapter opens is taken from an article which Peter Drucker wrote in the *Wharton Magazine* in 1976 entitled 'The bored board'. In it he said that all over the Western world boards were under attack and that the board had become 'an impotent ceremonial and legal fiction'. His broadside knew no bounds as, in the course of it, he claimed that Hermann Abs, the German banker, had sat on about 150 boards at the same time! In fact he held some thirty supervisory board posts, until the law named after him enforced a limit of ten. Be that as it may, Peter Drucker's description of the standing of boards of directors in the mid-1970s was both unflattering and to the point. Boards were too often seen as not being in control of their companies and as having failed to prevent either disasters or malpractices.

Boards are still in the firing line in Britain and America, often accused of not running their businesses as efficiently as they should and more generally of being answerable neither to their shareholders nor to society at large. The concern that boards do not work as they should, however, is widespread and is not confined just to company boards, but to boards of non-profit-making organisations as well. This raises issues for their chairmen. Are there, for example, better forms of board structure or changes to board procedures which would improve the functioning of boards? First, we need to examine more closely the criticisms levelled against boards and then to consider whether there are ways open to chairmen of meeting those criticisms.

Board failings

The most damaging charge made against boards is that they are ineffective. To quote an American source, Arch Patton and John Baker wrote in a 1987 *Harvard Business Review* article, 'We think the most serious indictment of boards lies in the inability of so many large US companies to compete in world markets.' The same indictment was made of boards of companies in Britain, as the country's share of world markets slid downwards. In addition to the central charge of incompetence, boards have been attacked for ignoring the interests of the shareholders, for being self-perpetuating bodies and for drawing their membership from too narrow a section of society.

Board legitimacy

The last three charges all relate to who is on the board and to how they got there. Since the composition of the board is the direct responsibility of the chairman, it is convenient to deal with these two questions together and first. The importance of how directors are elected relates to the role of the board as the source of authority within the company. The classical theory of the board is that the shareholders elect the directors and authorise them to run the company on their behalf. The board in its turn sets the aims of the enterprise and appoints managers to carry out those aims. The managers thus carry the authority of the board and the board that of the shareholders.

In practice, however, the shareholders of most public companies have little say in the appointment of directors, other than to nod through the nominations presented to them by the board. They can vote against the names which come up for election at the AGM, but it is made difficult for them to put forward alternative candidates. Provided that a company produces acceptable results, its board can in practice become self-perpetuating. The result is that the legitimacy of the board as the appointee of the shareholders, and therefore as carrying their authority, is based on something of a fiction. Once again the board, in Lord Caldecote's phrase, is marking its own examination papers.

Whether the authority of the directors and managers of the company stems as directly from the shareholders as the textbooks say that it should, may not be thought to have much practical relevance.

It is, however, all part of the charge that boards take too little account of the interests of the shareholders and are too far removed from shareholder influence. If board members feel that they owe their place on the board to the shareholders, they will be continually reminded of their responsibilities to them. If, in practice, they owe their place on the board to their fellow-directors, then they are dependent on how they stand with their colleagues rather than with the shareholders.

The lack of a keen and consistent sense of accountability to the shareholders is a basic reason why many boards have failed to achieve the results that they should have done. This lack of accountability stems from the inability or unwillingness of shareholders to exert any effective pressure on boards to improve their performance.

Board membership

A further consequence of boards being largely self-appointed is that too often they fail to look beyond their own circle in their search for outside directors. There are two arguments for enlarging the constituencies from which directors are chosen. One is that boards would thereby become more effective, and the other is that companies would be helped to identify their aims more clearly with those of the communities they serve. The two arguments overlap. For example, if there were more women on the boards of companies, then a larger pool of potential directorial talent would be being tapped and the make-up of boards would come more in line with that of the population as a whole.

An example from the United States of the first line of argument is the contention that boards are failing in their duty to their companies, because their directors have too much in common with each other and are therefore not prepared to be sufficiently critical. As the proportion of outsiders on American boards has gone up, so has the number who are active or retired executives of other companies, with the result that the majority of them see the issues which come before the board through managerial eyes.

In addition, many of these executives serve on each other's boards. A Senate Committee in the United States studied 130 companies and found that they had between them 12,500 interlocking directorships, both direct and indirect. A directly interlocking directorship is one where a director from company A sits on the board of company B and vice versa. An indirectly interlocking directorship occurs when directors from companies A and B both meet on the board of company C. The extent of the director network illustrated by these figures has, of course, to be seen against the background of the high proportion of outside directors on American boards. Nevertheless, the scale of the interchange between boards that the study throws up, raises questions about competition policy and about the relatively closed circle from which American companies draw their board members. Appointing directors from more varied backgrounds would be likely to lead to more challenge in board debates and would reduce the degree to which boards took in each other's washing.

Then there have been pressures, particularly in the United States, for more directors to be appointed from disadvantaged or minority groups. This is on the grounds of the second argument that boards should become more representative of the interests of the community. The Bullock Committee, to which I referred in the last chapter, followed the same approach in suggesting that the introduction of employee directors would make the boards of British companies more representative to the general good.

Increasing shareholder influence

There is clearly force in the arguments that boards are largely self-appointed and that their members tend to come from similar backgrounds. It is, however, important to disentangle the arguments about the balance of power in society from those which are directed at improving board effectiveness. On the latter point, strengthening the links between the board and the shareholders and ensuring that there are sufficient independent-minded, outside directors on boards should have an invigorating effect on board performance.

There are actions which chairmen can take and are taking to enable shareholders to exert more influence over the appointment of directors. One is to provide shareholders with relevant information about who is on the board, what their responsibilities are and what business experience they have had. Information on the backgrounds of those coming up for election at the AGM puts shareholders in a better position to judge how to cast their votes. Shareholders in their turn have an opportunity to let chairmen know their views on those up for election by writing their comments on their proxy forms. I used to study with care a summary of all the comments made by shareholders on their forms; they were instructive and often amusing as well. Individual shareholders have more influence than they probably imagine and should be more prepared to let chairmen know what they think of the company and of the way it is run.

While individual shareholders can convey their views, institutional shareholders can directly influence the composition of boards. The swing from private to institutional ownership of British companies has been dramatic; in 1968 institutions owned around one-third of Cadbury, ten years later they owned two-thirds of Cadbury Schweppes. Institutions have the resources to monitor who is on the boards of the companies in which they invest and to press for a body of directors which will bring the right mix of competence and challenge to the board.

Individual shareholders who are dissatisfied with the way in which a company is being run can sell their shares; the institutions collectively cannot. They have between them every incentive as shareholders to accept their responsibilities and to use their powers to ensure, for their own protection, that the companies in which they hold shares are properly run. A return to the position where the board is more directly accountable to the shareholders can therefore be brought about by the institutions.

The Committee on the Financial Aspects of Corporate Governance looked to the institutions for support in bringing about compliance with its recommendations and was encouraged to this end by the publication of the Institutional Shareholders Committee's report *The Responsibilities of Institutional Shareholders' in the UK*. The report specifically recommended that institutional investors should take a positive interest in the composition of boards of directors with particular reference to the following:

(i)   Concentrations of decision-making power not formally constrained by checks and balances appropriate to the particular company.

(ii) The appointment of a core of non-executives of appropriate calibre, experience and independence.

This recommendation was backed in the body of the report as follows:

> The composition of a company's Board must be a matter of legitimate concern to shareholders. They have the opportunity to confirm all appointments to the Board which are initiated by the existing directors, and there is a growing acceptance that a properly balanced Board is essential to the well-being of a company. Institutions individually, or where appropriate collectively, are increasingly prepared to suggest change to remedy perceived weaknesses and where necessary to encourage Boards to appoint an adequate number of independent non-executive directors. Institutional shareholders seek to identify serious deficiencies at an early stage, and to initiate appropriate action. The most effective action is taken quickly, and without publicity.

That call for swift and appropriate action represents a marked shift in the balance of power between shareholders and directors and, to the degree that it is followed, it will lead to a significant increase in board accountability.

Board candidates

When it comes to the question of whether boards look wide enough in their search for potential directors, that is squarely in the hands of chairmen. Chairmen are searching for the best people whom they can find for their boards, those who will add most value to the existing board team. It is, therefore, in their own interests to draw board candidates from as broad a range of sources as possible.

This is where a formal, systematic approach to identifying qualified board candidates has so much to offer to chairmen. Such an approach provides chairmen with a larger field to choose from and protects them against the criticism that their search for independent board members was not conducted with sufficient diligence and professionalism. By appointing outside directors from a variety of backgrounds, chairmen are aiming to improve the effectiveness of their boards and to make them more representative of the world outside the boardroom into the bargain. If, of course, representativeness were pursued as an end in itself, without due regard for efficiency, then it would qualify for addition to the list of causes of board incompetence.

A further reason for drawing board candidates from a wider pool than in the past is that boards nowadays have to spend an increasing proportion of their time looking outwards at the effects of their actions on the communities in which they carry on their businesses, at home and abroad. There is, therefore, a commercial case for having board members whose background and experience give them an understanding of how companies and their activities are perceived from the outside.

Ineffective boards

The main criticism of boards in Britain and in North America has been that they direct and control their businesses inadequately. One measure of collective inadequacy has been loss of share of world markets, another has been the unearthing of cases of company corruption. In addition, a number of sizeable companies have gone bankrupt, whose boards seem either to have been incapable of reversing the downward slide of their businesses or to have been unaware just how serious their situation was until it was too late. A dramatic account of what it is like to find that you have joined an ineffective board appeared in an article in the 1976 autumn edition of the *Harvard Business Review*. It was written by Louis Cabot, a Harvard professor, and it describes the collapse of Penn Central.

> I served for one fateful year on the Board of Penn Central. The education was fast, brutal and highly practical. Even today the lawsuits are not all settled and that education has cost me several times more than the price of a Harvard Business School tuition. At each Penn Central directors' meeting, which only lasted one and a half hours, we were presented with long lists of relatively small capital expenditures to approve; we were shown sketchy financial reports which were rarely discussed in any detail. The reports were not designed to be revealing, and we were asked not to take them away from the meeting. We always had an oral report by the Chief Executive Officer promising better results next month which never came true.

Louis Cabot did all the right things as an outside director, including writing to the chairman to say that this was no way to run a business. But before any of his letters had even been answered, Penn Central had collapsed and Cabot was sued along with the other directors.

What is clear from his vivid description of Penn Central board meetings is that the board simply failed to do its job. The board was both uninformed and misinformed. It exercised no real control over the CEO, because it did not provide itself with the means of doing so. It spent relatively little time on its considerable responsibilities and part of that time was given over to the discussion of irrelevant items of capital expenditure. The fault lay with the chairman and the board, but primarily with the chairman. It is for chairmen to set the agenda and it is part of their job to make sure that board members receive the information they need and that they receive it in time. Equally, it was for board members to press the CEO to produce the reports which they had to have in order to be able to keep him and the business on track.

The primary reason that companies get into serious financial difficulties is that their boards have allowed matters to drift. Drift is due to indecision and to the lack of timely, relevant information; the remedies for both lie in the hands of the chairman.

To return to the quotation from Peter Drucker, I see the failure of boards less as an institutional failure than as a human one. The Penn Central disaster was due to the board not carrying out the functions for which it was appointed. The criticism of boards for their ineffectiveness, as measured by a number of well-publicised company failures, is not so much a criticism of boards as institutions as an argument for making certain that boards work as they should. It is up to board chairmen and to the shareholders who appoint the board members to see that they do. Nevertheless, it is right to ask, in the wake of all the criticisms of the way in which boards function here and in the United States, whether there are other board models which might have structural or procedural advantages over the unitary board.

TWO-TIER BOARDS

The only other type of board whose working we can study on any scale is the European two-tier board, which was developed in its present form in Germany; historically, its form goes back to the Dutch trading companies of the seventeenth century. The importance of the two-tier board structure is that it is associated with a country with an impressive record of economic growth, and that moves to harmonise company law within the European Union may lead to pressures for its wider adoption. All that we are concerned with here are those aspects of the two-tier board approach which could be relevant to chairmen who are seeking ways of improving the effectiveness of unitary boards.

How two-tier boards work

A two-tier board fulfils the same basic functions as a unitary board. It is accountable to the shareholders for the direction and management of the company. It does so through a division of these responsibilities, between a supervisory board which oversees the direction of the company and a management board which runs the business. The supervisory board controls the management board through appointing its members and through its statutory right to have the final say on major decisions affecting the company. The structure rigorously separates the control function from the management function, and members of the one board cannot be members of the other.

Given that American boards are tending to increase their proportion of outside directors, it is sometimes said that they are moving towards creating a *de facto* two-tier structure, with a predominantly outside board performing the supervisory function and with an executive committee under it, made up wholly of executive directors, standing in for the management board. This is not an accurate analogy, however, and there are a number of important differences between a unitary board – even if most of its members are outside directors – and a supervisory board.

First, the unitary board, however many outsiders it has on it, remains in full control of every aspect of the company's activities. It initiates action and it sees that the action which it has initiated is carried out. All its directors, whether executive or outside directors, share the same aims and the same responsibilities. The supervisory board, on the other hand, may have to approve management action, but it is primarily a monitoring body, not an initiatory one. The tasks and duties of the two boards are different as are their legal responsibilities. Second, the chief executive at least will be on a unitary board, so the board combines outside and inside directors whereas the supervisory board does not. Third, the kind of people who are outside members of a unitary board will not be precisely the same as the members of a supervisory board; this is leaving on one side the possibility that some supervisory board members may have been appointed by the employees. This distinction arises because being an outside member of an operating board may require a different set of attributes from that of being a member of a strictly supervisory body.

Employee representation

At this point it would be as well to clear up any misunderstandings about the relationship between two-tier boards and the representation of employee interests. The two-tier board structure was introduced in Germany in the nineteenth century to strengthen the control of the shareholders over the companies in which they had invested. When the question of how employees could be given a greater say in the conduct of the enterprises in which they worked became a live political issue in Germany, the two-tier structure provided a means of meeting that aim at the highest level of governance. It enabled the interests of the employees to be represented on the supervisory board without involving them directly in the management control of the company. The two-tier board system has thus provided a channel for employee representation at board level, but that is not why it was devised. The arguments for separating the functions of supervision and of management are independent of those concerned with ways of representing the employee interest.

Similarly, the question of board representation of employees is independent of whether boards are unitary or two-tier. Employee directors sit on unitary boards in Sweden; British Steel and the British

Post Office have both had employee directors on their boards and the Chrysler Corporation has done the same in the United States. The other way round, supervisory boards in Holland do not have directors representing the employee interest on them, although all nominations to the supervisory board have to be acceptable both to the employees and to the shareholders.

Positive features of the two-tier structure

One advantage of the two-tier board structure is its clarity of purpose. The two functions of supervision and of management are kept absolutely distinct and they are carried out by different people. The dividing line between direction, which is the task of a unitary board, and management, which involves turning direction into action, is less clear-cut. When some of the same people are involved in both, the distinction becomes further blurred. Directors of supervisory and of management boards know precisely what their duties are and do not have to remember which of the two hats they are wearing.

As a result of having clear guidelines, both supervisory and management boards can concentrate their attention on their key tasks; their reporting relationships are well defined, as are the information needs of the supervisory board.

Supervisory board members are subject to election more directly and positively than most unitary board directors; since they appoint the management board members, the linkage between the owners, the monitors and the managers is clear and understood. The supervisory directors and the directors of the management board derive their authority from those who appoint them.

The supervisory board is also in a position to take an entirely independent view of the actions of management, since there is no overlap of membership between the two boards. Unitary board members owe their loyalty to the company, but they also have loyalties to their board colleagues; at times those two loyalties may pull against each other. There should be no such conflict of loyalties for supervisory board members.

As a last point, the two-tier board structure is able to accommodate the representation of interests other than those of the owners of the company, without interfering with the responsibility of the management for the running of the business. To the extent that representation of interests becomes an issue for boards, then the two-tier structure is better adapted to deal with it than the unitary structure.

Operating differences

There are significant operating differences between the two types of board structure. The first is that with a unitary board it is the board as a whole which is the driving force within the company. In the two-tier structure, it is the management board which is in the driving seat. The management board is responsible for developing the strategy for the business. The supervisory board may comment on, or suggest alternatives to, the plans for the future of the business put forward by the management board, but the initiative lies with the latter. Supervisory boards normally meet quarterly and so their ability to exert a positive influence on the management board and on the actual operations of the company is necessarily limited, although there are often informal ways of keeping at least the chairman of the supervisory board informed between meetings. Unitary boards meet more frequently and the combined energies of all board members can be focused on raising the level of attainment of their companies.

The second difference in operating practice is that there is little opportunity for interaction between the two boards in the development of policies. This follows from the strict separation of responsibilities between them and from the relative infrequency of supervisory board meetings. In a unitary board, strategies, plans and policies are developed over time, through debate and argument, within the board and between the board and the senior managers. This method of hammering out decisions through a dialogue between those who form policy and those who put it into effect seems to me a strength of the unitary approach.

The track record

European companies have been successful under both types of board structure and variants of them, so there are no obvious conclusions to be drawn from comparing on a wholesale basis the results of companies run by unitary boards and by two-tier boards. It would be difficult in any case to isolate that part of a company's improvement in performance which could be solely attributed to its board. It is equally hard to differentiate between the effectiveness of a form of organisation and that of the people who make it work. To take a practical example, how would the success of Japanese companies in general be apportioned as between their board structures, their decision-making systems outside the board, the commitment of their work-forces and the place of business in Japanese society?

It is because broad-brush comparisons can tell us little, that two recent publications on the workings of different types of board structure are of particular value to the corporate governance debate. *The Corporate Board*, by Demb and Neubauer, is based on research carried out at the International Institute for Management Development in Lausanne, involving interviews with 71 directors serving on more than 500 boards in 8 countries. Its conclusions are, therefore, drawn from practical experience across national boundaries. The authors' research brings out that, regardless of country or culture, the views of directors as to the role of the board are remarkably uniform. Their views, however, as to how boards should be involved in governance are remarkably diverse. The significant point is that this diversity of view applied 'even when directors were on the same board, or operated within the same national setting'.

Jonathan Charkham's *Keeping Good Company*, to which reference has already been made, gives an admirably lucid account of board systems in the United Kingdom, the United States, Japan, France and Germany. His book explains the governance framework within which boards in these different countries operate and the nature of the checks and balances to which they are subject. It describes the way in which companies are directed and controlled seen from the outside. *The Corporate Board* complements this approach by looking at governance from within, from the point of view of board members themselves.

In the meantime, what lessons can be drawn from the workings of two-tier boards, which could be relevant to unitary board chairmen?

CONCLUSIONS

Adopt the two-tier system?

The first conclusion I would draw is that nothing would be gained by attempting to impose a common two-tier board structure throughout the European Union. This is partly because such structural advantages as it does have are not decisive in terms of operating results. It is also because two-tier boards and unitary boards are but parts of integrated business systems, which have evolved to suit their particular economic and social environments. A great deal more than the structure of the board would have to be changed to graft the two-tier approach successfully on to a company previously run by a unitary board. A further point is that it is simple to change the boxes on an organisation chart, but quite a different matter to change the way in which people work. The trap over trying to alter board systems by fiat is that the structure may change to comply with the law, but the chances are that the working of the system will carry on as before.

Clarify the board's role

I would, however, suggest that two features of the two-tier structure should be taken note of – the clarity of its design and the independence of the supervisory board – and that the aim should be to build them into the unitary structure. Taking clarity of design and purpose first, the unitary board provides considerable scope for confusion over what the duties of directors to the company entail, over where the division lies between direction and management, and over the executive director's responsibilities as a director and as a manager. All of which implies that time devoted by chairmen to ensuring the agreement of their boards, regarding their functions and how these should be carried out, would be well spent.

Equally, there should be formal methods of induction for newly appointed board members, rather than an expectation that they should pick the job up as they go along. The fact that the unitary structure is less well defined than the two-tier structure means that more effort has to be put in to pinning down exactly what the role of a unitary board member is. There is no substitute for setting such definitions down on paper, hard though it is for chairmen to do.

Strengthen board independence

Dealing next with independence, the members of the supervisory board are well placed to carry out their monitoring function on behalf of the shareholders, because they are independent of the management. Their only link with the management is that they appoint the members of the management board, and so to that extent they have an interest in backing their appointees. The supervisory directors can exercise full control over the management proposals which come to them, because they are not already committed to those proposals in any way. The problem with a unitary board is that by the time projects reach board level for approval, the executive commitment to them may be such that the independent board members can hardly do other than to go along with them.

Actions which chairmen are able to take to strengthen the independence of decision of a unitary board, in the interests of the shareholders, include having sufficient independent directors of the right kind on the board and making certain that the board's power of decision is not pre-empted. Pre-emption can be avoided by ensuring that proposals come to the board at an early enough stage in the decision-making process. This is one of a chairman's more difficult responsibilities.

Too often, a persuasive case for a single course of action is put to a board, as if there were no rational alternative. The presentation may include other less compelling options, in order to steer board members towards the preferred solution. For outside directors to challenge the executive directors, at this stage in the decision-making process, could result in confrontation and in an unacceptable degree of delay. The only way to avoid pre-emption of this kind is for chairmen to ensure that proposed lines of action and their alternatives are discussed in principle at the board, before a major management commitment is made to any one of them. Board members then have the opportunity to influence which possibilities should be worked on by the management team and to ensure that they have a genuine choice between properly documented projects, rather than having that choice made for them.

What counts is the way boards work

The basic structure of the unitary board does not seem to me to lie at the heart of the problem. The question marks arise over the membership of unitary boards and over the way in which they function. Unitary boards have shown themselves capable of directing businesses competently, of setting high standards of conduct, of being responsive to shareholders and of taking account of society's needs. To do all of this they have to be properly led and they have to have committed directors on them – directors who can give enough time to meet the demands imposed by the arduous task of directing a business efficiently.

It is the responsibility of the shareholders, and particularly of the main institutions among them, to assure themselves that the companies in which they have invested are headed by effective boards of this kind. It is the responsibility of chairmen to ensure that their boards match up to the legitimate expectations of their shareholders.

CHAPTER 5

CHAIRING THE BOARD

The effort made by a chairman to ensure that meetings
are properly conducted may well be the most valuable
contribution he makes to the good of his company.
Stanley Dixon, *Accountants Digest*

TAKING THE CHAIR

The primary task of chairmen is to chair their boards. This is what
they have been appointed to do and, however the duties at the top of
a company may be divided, chairing the board is their responsibility
alone. The law may only be concerned with the need for there to be
a chairman, but board members are concerned with finding the most
competent chairman they can, for the good of the company and to
ensure that the time which they spend at meetings should be as
productive as possible. I agree with Stanley Dixon's conclusion with
which this chapter opens, and chairmen of any kind of enterprise will
find his notes on the art of chairing a meeting helpful. Taking the chair
at board meetings is the aspect of the job of chairmen which is furthest
from the public eye, but the one where their personal contribution is
decisive.

It is decisive because to obtain full value from a meeting of any kind
is a difficult task. While diligent preparation beforehand by the
chairman is essential, there is no way of knowing in advance just how
a meeting will develop. We are talking about a collective process and
a dynamic one. Everything turns on the way in which people react to
the ideas under discussion and to each other. The job of the chairman
is to encourage board members to give of their individual best in a
co-operative cause.

Analogies which liken chairmen to conductors are helpful, but can
be carried too far. Conductors at least have a score to work to and

they expect their orchestras to be doing the same. Chairmen have to be their own composers and they cannot be sure in advance what tunes their soloists will play, or whether they will perform at all. Where the analogy is to the point is that chairmen, like conductors, are responsible for the success of the performance and to succeed they have to be in control from start to finish. As another authority on chairing committees, John Tropman, pointed out in *Directors and Boards* (Summer, 1980): 'Committees in trouble have several directors directing at the same time from the same seat.'

MEETINGS OF THE BOARD

Aims of the meeting

The aim of a board meeting is for the board to arrive at the soundest conclusions it can on those matters with which it has to deal. This requires all board members to contribute as pertinently as they are able to the discussion. The resource which chairmen have to hand is the time and the talents of their board members. If they can encourage their directors to participate in the board's work to the best of their ability, then the board will be giving the company the leadership that it deserves and board members will feel that their valuable time has been well spent.

The opportunity which a board meeting offers is that of debating the issues before it and of arriving, through collective effort, at better conclusions – better from the company's point of view – than would have been possible without that debate. The board is a deliberative council and it is also the top decision-making body in the company; therefore only those matters which need to go to the summit should be taken there. Equally, a summit commands a wide view and it is precisely this breadth of view which a board should bring to the matters under scrutiny.

The aim which chairmen have continually in mind is that of coming to the best conclusion in the circumstances, not simply reaching an acceptable conclusion. To achieve this, chairmen have to control the discussion in order to keep it to the point, while at the same time encouraging board members who feel they have something worth saying to take part in the debate. This is a difficult balance to hold, because interventions which may not appear to be quite on target may nevertheless be picked up by others and developed usefully. It is from the to and fro of discussion that new ways forward will emerge. The purpose of a board meeting is to enable board members to build on each other's analyses and ideas. The chairman's task is to keep the discussion moving forward until it has achieved all that it can, then to bring matters to a conclusion and to ensure that the conclusion is acted upon.

Place of meeting

It may seem strange to move straight from the purpose of a board meeting to the subject of where meetings should be held. But given that this is the meeting of the company's summit, every effort should be made to ensure that such meetings are as productive as possible. What I find quite extraordinary is how often board meetings are held in inadequate places under unsuitable conditions. I have attended board meetings in rooms which were not properly ventilated, so that the choice was between fresh air and intrusive noise, or quiet and stuffiness leading inexorably to somnolence. I have sat at rectangular board tables, where those on the wings on the same side of the table could never see each other, nor hear each other for half of the time. There is a curious tendency for those who find it hardest to hear to gravitate to the extremities of any meeting table. It seems to me absurd to invest in the services of the best board members you can muster and then fail to invest in providing them with productive surroundings in which to meet.

The rules are straightforward. Board members should be able to see each other and hear each other without effort. If some form of microphonic gadgetry is necessary for those taking part to be audible, either the board is too big or the room is unsuitable. To get the most out of a debate, it is essential for the participants to be able to see each other. How people express themselves is often as important as what they have to say, because facial expressions and gestures communicate just as words do. Equally, it is only by watching speakers as well as listening to them that you can decide when they are coming to the end of what they have to say, or have reached the point when they perhaps ought to be doing so. For chairmen to be in control they have to be in a position to see all the participants, which is why I prefer oval or round tables, or a horseshoe arrangement of seating.

The room should be quiet and the ventilation good. If you want board members to give of their best, you make it as easy as possible for them to concentrate on the matters in hand, from the beginning to the end of the meeting. I favour having no breaks so that the meeting can continue without interruption, with board members helping themselves to whatever refreshments will keep them alert and involved, but with no other distractions. Proper lighting is also important; seating people to face glare through windows may be an accepted negotiating tactic, but it is not one which should be inflicted on colleagues.

Board members are individuals and it is up to the chairman and to the board secretary to give thought as to where each should sit and to find out their preferences – do they prefer to sit always in the same place or between the same people, or would they rather move around? I took to arriving at one meeting early in order to change the place names if necessary, so as not to have to sit next to a good friend who was a dedicated smoker of Gauloises. Then I resolved the problem by settling the seating arrangements with the company secretary. Lastly, chairs should be a match with the table and should not distract through being uncomfortable.

Many of these points may sound as if they are of small account, but they are not. Chairmen and company secretaries have only to reflect on the cost of board meetings, in terms of the people involved and of their value to the company, to see why they must apply themselves imaginatively to providing their boards with a good working environment.

As a separate point, there are a variety of aids to communication which board members may want to use, from overhead projectors to screens for films or videos. What matters is that they should carry out their respective functions efficiently and unobtrusively. They are there to assist the discussion and not to detract from it by failing to work, or by requiring a rearrangement of people or furniture before they can be brought into action. As a director of IBM in Britain, I have had the privilege of meeting in a board room where all such devices were built in and an integral part of the design of the meeting-place. Again, this seems to be a thoroughly justified investment.

Timing of meetings

There is less to be said on timing, other than that meetings should be started on time and that they should have an agreed finishing time, either at a specific hour or in line with a specific event like lunch. A bank used to have as good a system for starting board meetings on time as I have yet come across. They paid a fee for attendance at meetings and the total fees for all board members were put ready beforehand on the board table. As soon as the hour for the meeting struck, the total amount was divided between those who were then present.

After a point, meetings become progressively less effective, and two-and-a-half to three hours is as long as it is reasonable to expect board members to play their part enthusiastically and to the full. If a board meeting needs to be longer than that, it is sensible to continue with a second, separate meeting.

As important as the total time for the meeting is the time spent on each agenda item. At one series of meetings which I chaired, the secretary used to put an indicative number of minutes against each point on the agenda. I think that is attempting to impose too strict a pattern on the proceedings. But it is right that the chairman should start the meeting with a rough idea of the time to be allowed for each of the main items, leaving everything else to be dealt with in whatever time remains. It is logical to clear matters of report first and then to come on to matters of substance in their order of priority.

Agenda

This leads on to the agenda. The board secretary and the chairman prepare the agenda, in consultation with the chief executive, who will know what decisions are needed from the board so as not to hold up the running of the business. Setting the agenda is one of the ways in which the chairman exercises control over the meeting. It is important that the matters to be discussed at a board meeting are signalled by the agenda. This gives directors the chance to reflect on them in advance. It also means that directors who are going to miss meetings can let the chairman know beforehand what their views are on the subjects up for discussion. Directors could feel justifiably aggrieved if matters which were not on the agenda, and on which they had views to express, were dealt with in their absence.

Agenda items for board meetings come under three main headings. There are *matters of report* which keep the board informed about the company's progress. Such reports deal with matters which are the responsibility of the management, not the board, but they are essential to the board in the carrying-out of its monitoring function. Periodic reports on sales, profits, shares of market and cash-flow come under this heading. The reported figures may have implications which are proper matters for board debate, but it is for chairmen to keep the debate to those grounds and not to allow it to stray into advice from the outside directors to the management on how they should do their job.

As an example, having spent my working life in the food industry, I appreciate only too well the fascination which consumer advertising holds for board members. It is a subject on which everyone is expert; yet the death-knell to good advertising – that is, advertising which will achieve its purpose – is to allow board members any say whatsoever in its execution. That is a management function. But there is a policy aspect to advertising, which is a proper matter for the board to discuss and on which to rule. For advertising is part of the public face of a company and it has consequences for the company's identity and for the way in which the company is perceived by the community.

Therefore, a board should be aware of the advertising which is going out in the name of the company and it is entitled to take a view on whether the overall impact of that advertising is in keeping with the standards of the company or not. Advertising policy is a matter for the board; advertising execution is the responsibility of management. The line between policy and execution is not always easy to draw in practice, but it is up to the chairman to protect the management from board interference in matters which have been delegated to them.

After matters of report come *matters for decision*. They may be formalities like sealings, or they may be issues of critical importance like a bid for another company, the raising of funds or an appointment to a key post. The chairman will know which of these decisions have to be taken at any particular meeting and will ensure that board members are equally aware of the time constraints. There is a good deal to be said for having a preliminary discussion of an important issue and so drawing all the points of view on it from around the board table into the open. Board members then come to the next meeting prepared to bring the matter to a conclusion, but having reflected in the meantime on what was said the first time round.

This leads on to my third heading, which is the general one of *matters which need airing*, or on which the executives are looking to the board for a steer. It might be, for example, that pressure was being brought to bear on the company over an environmental issue. This would not be a matter for the board to deal with itself. It would, however, be for the board to advise what order of importance should be attached to the demands being made on the company, and whether the matter should run its normal managerial course or whether some special form of response was required.

One particular task which should never be given to boards is that of drafting. The board's advice on drafts is invaluable and I have never known a written statement which was not improved as a result of submitting it to the board and listening to their views. Drafting itself, however, is best done by an individual. When companies have a statement of note to make publicly, it should be drafted by one person, preferably by the chairman, with the advice and help of whomsoever they choose.

Board information

In deciding on the board agenda, the board secretary and the chairman also agree what information board members should receive in support of the items on it. The board's absolute requirement for timely and relevant information has already been stressed; without it no board can be in control. Reports should be presented in a consistent form to save the time of board members and to enable straightforward comparisons to be made, against the past or against forecast. The presentation of information can always be improved and board members need to be encouraged to express their views on presentation to the secretary or to the finance director. For example, I find it confusing if the figures read chronologically from left to right in one report and from right to left in another. It is all to do with accounting conventions but, when reports are going to the board, the sole test is whether they convey the essential information clearly and concisely to those who are due to receive them.

In providing board members with the information which they require in order to take decisions, the same considerations apply. The particular point to keep in mind under this heading is that the outside members of the board should not be at an unnecessary disadvantage to the executive members. This may mean giving them some additional background information on why, for example, the company has reached the point where a particular decision is necessary.

Board reports have to be understandable to the non-expert and should provide only the information which is needed to debate the relevant issue intelligently and to come to a judgement on it. Anything more risks obscuring the key points and reduces the chance of the document being read in full. Rudyard Kipling cut every word out of his writings which he judged to be unnecessary; this meant that he intended every word he left in to be read. He should be the model for those who draft board papers. Equally, the chairman should take it for granted that board papers have been thoroughly studied before the meeting. Nothing deadens a discussion as effectively as opening it with a rehearsal of what the majority of board members have already read.

It is part of the job of chairmen to go through the board papers, as if they were outside directors, to ensure that they provide board members with all the information which they need for the proper discharge of their responsibilities.

The course of the meeting

The chairman needs to decide with the chief executive and the board secretary what it is that the board meeting has to achieve. What decisions are required, by when, and on what matters are the management looking to the board for a lead? The chairman's objective is to arrive at the best outcome in respect of each deliberative item on the agenda and to do so by drawing on the collective wisdom of those sitting round the board table. The chairman will ask the appropriate director to introduce each item for discussion and then open the matter up for debate. The chairman's job is to keep the discussion on track, without discouraging the introduction of lateral ideas which may stimulate new lines of thought.

The Bishop of Ely in preaching at the memorial service for a wise and much-loved Cambridge don said of him: 'A committee's time, with him in the chair, was not time to be wasted, the Chairman's task [being] to hold it to the question needing resolution now (his perception of where that question lay was perhaps his own distinctive brilliance).' That sums up the chairman's task admirably. The chairman has to perceive what needs to be resolved and to keep the discussion moving – moving forward towards that resolution.

This demands an unrelenting concentration on what is being said and it also means making certain that valid points which have been raised are not passed by, just because the main stream of the discussion has taken a different course. Sound points can easily slip from sight as a discussion proceeds, but they need to be addressed and to be built on, and it is for chairmen to see that they are. Equally, chairmen have to avoid valuable time being wasted through misunderstandings. These can arise either from unequal knowledge between directors of the subject in hand, or from the failure of board members to make their points clearly. Chairmen are in the best position to sense both what a speaker meant and how it might have been interpreted by fellow board members. A timely intervention by the chairman can avoid those discussions at cross-purposes, which are entirely unproductive and, perhaps because of that, can generate quite unnecessary heat.

Chairmen who want to make the best use of the abilities of their boards aim to promote an atmosphere of openness at board meetings and to make certain that all directors are equally encouraged to express their views. Openness and equality between board members are essential to a thorough debate and chairmen have to work persistently for their achievement. This is particularly so when there are executives, in addition to the chief executive, on a board.

In a management meeting presided over by the chief executive, the executives are being chaired by the person to whom they report and this affects the nature of the discussion at such meetings. The danger is that executive directors may treat a board meeting as if it were a management meeting. It is for chairmen, by the way in which they handle a discussion, to affirm the equality of all board members, whether executive or outside directors, since they carry the same responsibilities. It is only when executive directors are confident that their standing in the boardroom is on a level with that of the chief executive that they are in a position to speak and to act as full directors.

I found an interesting comment on this matter of establishing the equality of board members in M. B. Brodie's booklet, published in 1963, on *The Committee Concept and Business*:

> This leads to a neglected but particularly important reason why the chairman of a business committee must be a man of outstanding calibre. Only through his own values, personality and skill can he develop and sustain a high level of morale and mutual respect amongst members in a committee, irrespective of status or the authority relationships which apply outside the committee.

For directors to feel that everyone is equal in the boardroom they have to acquire trust and confidence in their chairman and in the board. Trust and confidence are built on openness and on the willingness of all board members to say what they think, even if it may be critical of colleagues and of their proposals. Openness between board members is not only fundamental to the working of an effective board, it also sets the tone for relationships throughout the company.

Sir Walter Puckey writes: 'Complete freedom to speak under a reasonably independent chairman is a precious asset' (*The Board-Room*, p. 106). Complete freedom to speak is the goal to which chairmen, who appreciate the value of board discussions, are always working.

Board decisions

When there are matters before the board that require a decision, then that is the end which the chairman will have in view in controlling the discussion. Chairmen are not necessarily working to achieve consensus, although consensus strengthens decisions; they are seeking the best possible decisions in the interests of their company, and those may be decisions which do not command universal support. Chairmen determine when to bring discussions to an end and they sum up where their boards stand, if there is a need to do so. It may be that there is insufficient agreement to reach a conclusion, in which case the chairman has to decide how to achieve the breadth of agreement which will be needed, if the matter is to be settled at the next meeting.

Voting is an unsatisfactory way of resolving an issue over which the board is divided: to quote Sir Walter Puckey again, 'Voting is a concession to weak chairmanship' (1969, p. 198). I have known a chairman end every discussion by going round the board table asking each director for their view; this is an equally weak form of chairmanship. It is for chairmen to judge the feeling of the meeting and to put propositions to their fellow board members which reflect that feeling. Chairmen are there to give a lead, not to count heads.

Minutes

The decisions arrived at by the board are recorded in the minutes. They are the authority for action and therefore their wording is important. Their wording is also important because they constitute, along with any board papers filed with the minutes, the record of the meeting. A nice judgement is required as to how full a record should be kept. The Cadbury board minutes only recorded decisions and not discussion, and directors' initials were put against all minutes requiring action. Directors received copies of those minutes which had their initials on them, and those minutes were both their marching orders and their authority for action.

There are times, however, when it could be important for future directors to have some background to a decision, such as how the need for the decision arose in the first place. This may best be done by filing a background brief with the minutes, rather than by extending the minutes.

Individual directors may ask for their dissension to a decision to be recorded in the minutes. This does not alter the responsibility of all members to support decisions arrived at in the board, regardless of their personal views. But it suggests either that the directors concerned see the need to protect their position, or that they may at a later stage use their dissent to undermine someone else's position.

Whatever the reason, a recorded dissent is a signal which chairmen will take seriously.

The possibility that the minutes of the board might be used in evidence against it, by one of the authorities with jurisdiction over companies, has tended to make minutes briefer and less informative than they were when they were written for internal use only. From the point of view of anyone interested in business history, this is a loss. But it is the inevitable result of the greater degree of external control now exercised over companies and the more frequent incidence of legal suits. Chairmen's memoirs are no substitute for well-drafted minutes backed by the board papers to which they refer.

Chairmen and company secretaries are right to take considerable care over the minutes, which should be circulated as promptly as practicable. The perfunctory way in which minutes are usually dealt with at the beginning of board meetings reflects little appreciation of the time spent in preparing them.

The chairman's approach

Up to this point, I have referred to chairmen rather as if they were impartial judges, listening to the points of view expressed, keeping the discussion relevant and then summing up the board's conclusions. The chairman has to be impartial in the sense of seeing that all board members who have something worth saying say it and that executive rank or seniority do not undermine the equality of all directors.

Chairmen, however, are as equal as other board members and as entitled to have their own views on the matters under discussion; to that extent they are partial and take part in the debate. The more that chairmen are looked to as representing their companies as well as their boards, the more likely they are to have their personal views on the course which their companies should take. How do they square their own convictions on a particular matter with their task as chairmen to ensure an entirely open debate?

The two positions are reconcilable, provided that chairmen enter the debate prepared to accept their board's judgement and that they are seeking through debate the best possible outcome for the issues under discussion. These provisos are necessary because there are chairmen who regard their boards as rubber stamps. They know what decisions they want to arrive at before the meeting starts, and the directors foregather simply to endorse the conclusions of the chairman or the chief executive.

At one such board, an outside director who queried an acquisition proposal was told that, if the directors were going to get into that kind of detail, board meetings would have to start at breakfast time! Such chairmen do not believe that discussion at the board can contribute anything to executive decisions; their boards are ornamental and serve no useful deliberative purpose. Autocratic chairmanship of that kind turns the board into an executive committee.

As chairman, I held views with varying degrees of tenacity on most of the issues coming before the board. I also believed that subjecting those views to debate at the board would result in their being improved upon and usually modified. It is only through a thorough debate that you can be sure that all the options have surfaced. However apparently clear-cut an executive proposal may seem, new angles to it nearly always emerge when it is discussed at the board. If the original executive proposition comes through intact, then it has been well tested and its initiator can be confident of its merits.

I mentioned in passing the importance of bringing all the options to the surface. One of my concerns as chairman was to encourage the executives to consider every possible way of tackling a problem, however much that might involve challenging accepted beliefs. The danger is that somewhere in the process of framing executive proposals an idea will be thought to be too radical – 'the chairman will never wear it'. There is no way of knowing what chairmen will wear until you try it on them, and I suspect that too often imaginative proposals are not aired for fear that they may offend the chairman's or the company's basic beliefs. This is an important reason why chairmen should encourage openness of debate.

What if the chairman or the chief executive disagrees with a proposal which is coming before the board? Clearly it depends on how fundamental the disagreement is. If the issue was one about which the chairman or the chief executive felt so strongly that they would resign should the board go against them, then they must make their position clear before the discussion starts. In that extreme instance, the debate will be about their position rather than the issue which gave rise to it.

The much more common situation is that there is simply a difference of view prior to the matter being discussed at the board. For example, it may be that the finance director is proposing that the company should raise more funds and I, as chairman, have doubts about whether this is an opportune time to do so. I would tell the finance director in advance that I was not convinced by his proposal, so that he knew where I stood. He would then put his proposal to the board and I, as a board member, would have the opportunity to express my views on it along with everyone else. But it has to be clear that, in disagreeing with the finance director, I will, as chairman, accept the board's view when we have argued the matter out. Interventions by chairmen cannot be reconciled with their duty to encourage an open debate, if they put their views so forcibly at the outset as to pre-empt discussion.

The outcome of a finely balanced debate can be affected by the order in which those for or against a proposal speak; and the decision by chairmen when to bring individual board members into a particular debate is one aspect of their control of the meeting. This, in turn, makes the point that chairmen need to know their board members as individuals and as much as possible about the way in which their minds work. Some may have to be encouraged to express their views, even on an issue where their experience is likely to be relevant, others may have to be restrained. It is not only that the opinions of particular board members may be of value at a given point in a debate, they may also have the ability to stimulate new ideas in others.

This stress on the way in which an effective board works as a collective explains why the composition of the board is so crucial. A potential outside director could have just the right career experience, but be unsuitable because of his or her personality. The chairman has to judge in putting forward the name, say, of a particularly forceful person, whether their participation would encourage discussion among other board members or kill it.

The longer board members have been together, the more they will have established their own methods of working as a group and the more important it may become to add new members who will be constructively critical of established views. Because the personal chemistry of board members is so crucial, it is difficult for unitary boards to accommodate new members who are wished on them, for example as representatives of outside interests. New directors need to be nominated and appointed with the involvement and agreement of all the existing board members.

COMMITTEES OF THE BOARD

Finance committee

One of the ways in which chairmen prevent board meetings from becoming overloaded, and either going on too long or requiring discussion to be curtailed, is by setting up appropriate committees of the board. For example, many companies have finance committees to go through the detail of financial proposals which are beyond the authority of the executives, and to make recommendations on them to the full board. This meets the test of focusing the board's attention on those issues with which it alone can deal and leaving any preliminary work to be carried out at a lower level. As company chairman, I chaired a finance committee of the board. This kept me in close touch with the financial state of the business, on which I had to report to the shareholders.

The two points which I kept in mind as chairman of the finance committee were, first, that the committee should remain strictly a finance committee, concerning itself with the financial consequences of executive proposals, not with the merits of the proposals themselves. There is a danger that a committee of this kind, if it has the chairman and the chief executive on it, can become an unofficial executive committee of the board.

Second, I made sure that the committee did not interfere in the management of the business. It went into financial matters in some detail, but this was to assist the board in coming to its conclusions, not to second-guess the finance director. Finally, the committee had delegated authority to agree certain levels of capital expenditure, again to relieve the board of unnecessary detail.

One reason for forming board committees is to make the board's task more manageable; another is to enable the outside directors to play their full part in the direction of the company. It will take outside directors some time to understand the company and something of the people who make it up, if their only point of contact is through meetings of the board. Committees of the board provide outside directors with a structure through which to gain a greater grasp of the business and give them a role beyond that of attending board meetings.

Audit committee

An effective audit committee provides an important assurance to shareholders – and to chairmen – that a key aspect of a board's duties will be rigorously discharged. Since 1978, the New York Stock Exchange has required all listed companies to have audit committees made up solely of independent, outside directors. The American Treadway Commission, in its 1987 report, concluded that audit committees played a crucial role in ensuring the integrity of US corporate financial reporting. Even where they might have been set up mainly to meet listing requirements, American experience has shown that audit committees soon proved their worth and developed into essential committees of the board.

The Committee on the Financial Aspects of Corporate Governance followed the American lead and recommended that all companies listed on the London Stock Exchange should establish audit committees. Specimen terms of reference for audit committees were published as an appendix to the report, by way of guidance. Some of the Committee's further recommendations were as follows:

- Audit committees should be formally constituted to ensure that they have a clear relationship with the boards to whom they are answerable and to whom they should report regularly.
- They should normally meet at least twice a year.
- Only outside non-executive directors should be members; the minimum membership should be three, the majority of whom must be independent.
- The external auditor should normally attend audit committee meetings, as should the finance director and the head of internal audit.

The audit committee recommendations formed an important part of the Committee's Code of Best Practice. They set the minimum number of outside directors, and more significantly of independent outside directors, that boards needed to have if they were to comply with the Code. From a board chairman's point of view, an effective audit committee ensures that a thorough review of audit matters will be carried out, that the outside directors will be able to play a positive part in the work of the board in a field where their independence of judgement will be of particular value, and that the auditors will have direct access to the outside directors.

The effectiveness of an audit committee turns on the competence of its chairman and the calibre of the outside directors available to make up its membership. Those called to serve on an audit committee require commitment, training and skill. They do not have to be financially qualified, but they do have to have enough understanding of audit matters to know what questions to ask and how to evaluate the answers.

The terms of reference of an audit committee are key, if the board is to retain full collective responsibility for financial reporting and control, and if the committee is not to involve itself in too much detail. To avoid this, it may be helpful to include a short sentence on what the audit committee is *not* there to do – that is to say, to delve into the management of the business.

The terms of reference of the audit committee which I chaired ended with the following statement:

> The Audit Committee shall not be responsible for reviewing executive decisions nor for monitoring the efficiency of the management.

Chairman's committee

At Cadbury Schweppes, I chaired what was entitled the chairman's committee – referred to in Chapter 3. It dealt with those matters which remuneration and nomination committees would cover in North America. The committee was made up of all the outside directors, with the chief executive attending as necessary. It discussed every proposal for board membership, whether of executive or of outside directors, before putting nominations to the board as a whole. The committee proposed names after thorough debate and after taking whatever professional advice was appropriate.

The committee also agreed the pay of the executive directors, the operation of the share option scheme and any other matters which affected directors' remuneration or conditions of employment. An example of the duties undertaken by the chairman's committee is as follows: the committee was responsible for nominating the new chief executive to the board on the retirement of his predecessor and for nominating my successor as chairman. Both appointments emphasised the value to the company and to the shareholders of having a group of experienced, independent directors on the board. The appointment of the chief executive required a decision as between the best internal and external candidates; it is hard to see how a wholly executive board could have exercised the same kind of informed but objective judgement over a decision of that kind.

Nowadays, both directors' remuneration and board nominations would be dealt with more formally and usually separately. The Committee on the Financial Aspects of Corporate Governance recommended that boards should appoint remuneration committees, made up wholly or mainly of outside directors and chaired by an outside director, and that executive directors should play no part in decisions on their own remuneration. The Committee stressed the importance of disclosure and of providing a full and clear statement of directors' present and future benefits and of the way in which they had been determined.

Directors' pay has become a public issue in Britain, and institutional shareholders have prepared guidelines of their own in regard to certain aspects of remuneration. Chairmen will, therefore, want to ensure that the approach of their boards to the fixing of the remuneration packages of directors will hold up well under public scrutiny. They will also need to decide whether they, or the chairmen of their remuneration committees – if that is not themselves wearing another hat – should answer questions on pay at the AGM.

Nomination committees are less well established in Britain than they are in the United States, and some companies would use their remuneration committees for the purpose. The Committee on the Financial Aspects of Corporate Governance's advice on the matter reads as follows:

> One approach to making board appointments, which makes clear how these appointments are made and assists boards in making them, is through the setting up of a nomination committee, with the responsibility of proposing to the board, in the first instance, any new appointments, whether of executive or non-executive directors.

The Committee's emphasis was on the need for a formal process for board appointments and for involving the board as a whole. Chairmen have a more straightforward task in explaining to shareholders and employees how directors are selected, if a properly constituted nomination committee is in place.

The aim of forming committees of the board is to assist the board to make the best use of its time and that of its members to ensure that the summit meeting concentrates on summit issues. In the past, board chairmen would have been the natural choice as chairmen of committees of the board. Now it would be more usual for them to assign the chairmanship of audit and remuneration committees to senior outside directors, while taking the chair at a nomination committee, provided they were not chief executives as well as chairmen. The essential point is that board committees should not usurp the functions of the board as a whole or become inner cabinets of the board. To avoid this danger, board committees should have clear terms of reference, and their terms of reference and membership should be reviewed annually. It is for their chairmen to make sure that they stick to their briefs.

THE CHAIRMAN'S AUTHORITY

Chairmen are put in charge of boards by their colleagues to ensure that board meetings will be run efficiently and that their time will not be wasted. Board members expect the chairman to exercise the degree of control needed to complete the board agenda in the accepted time and to arrive at the best conclusions of which the board is collectively capable. As long as chairmen use their authority impartially, with a view to expediting the business of the board, they will have the full support of their colleagues. Where the remaining directors can help is by keeping their fellow board members in line informally, so that it does not always fall to the chairman to enforce discipline.

What board members are looking for from their chairmen is that they should command their respect. Chairmen win the respect of their boards by preparing for meetings conscientiously and by their concentration and control during meetings. They have to be ready to listen carefully to everything that is said, and listening is an underrated accomplishment. They need to extract from a discussion what it is that the speakers really mean, which points are relevant to the matter in hand and how they can be used to come not just to a conclusion, but to as good a conclusion as possible. Chairmen who can lead their boards, rather than driving them, to arrive at balanced judgements will have earned the respect of their colleagues. The final requirement is that chairmen should not take themselves entirely seriously – a certain sense of the absurd is in order.

CHAPTER 6

THE CHAIRMAN AND THE CHIEF EXECUTIVE

There are probably as many ways of being a chairman
as there are chairmen themselves.
Heidrick and Struggles, p. 6

THE CHAIRMAN'S ROLE

The above conclusion from the survey conducted by Heidrick and
Struggles among more than eighty chairmen of British companies has
to be kept firmly in mind throughout. The role of chairman is one
which individual holders of the post have to establish for themselves.
The question which chairmen need to ask is whether the role, which
they have chosen or which others have tailored for them, is the one
which makes the most of their own abilities and those of their boards.
Attempting to answer that question brings out two key aspects of the
chairman's role.

First, chairmen are the leaders of their board teams and so their role
cannot be defined in isolation from the roles of the other members of
the team. Chairmen are concerned with the effectiveness of their
boards as a whole and their task is to provide whatever form of
leadership is needed to bring out the best in their board teams. Second,
the team members will change through time as will the challenges
facing their companies; thus the role of their chairmen does not remain
fixed from appointment to retirement. Chairmen change too as they
gather experience or move towards handing over to a successor. One
of the fundamental questions about the composition of boards is
whether they include someone who can talk openly to the chairman
about their chairmanship.

I am conscious of the importance of seeing board relationships as
a whole and of the way in which the pattern of a chairman's job
changes through time, because I have worked in a number of different

combinations of posts at the head of a company. I was chairman and managing director of Cadbury Group Ltd from 1965 to 1969, when Cadbury and Schweppes merged. I then became deputy chairman and managing director of Cadbury Schweppes Ltd, until I succeeded Lord Watkinson as chairman in 1974. During my fifteen years as chairman of Cadbury Schweppes plc, I shared the responsibility for the development of the business with two chief executives and three deputy chairmen, one of whom was also chief executive.

Although I have practical experience of different ways of splitting the top jobs, it is in the narrow context of one business as it grew. My comments, therefore, on the relationship between chairmen and their board colleagues are no more than that. They are comments to provoke thought and discussion, in the hope that such discussion will help chairmen decide what division of responsibilities at the top will best meet the needs of their particular situation. While the focus is on the separation or combination of the posts of chairman and of chief executive, that does not mean that the importance of other board positions, especially that of the deputy chairman, should be overlooked.

It is logical, however, to concentrate in this chapter on the respective roles of chairmen and of chief executives before broadening the discussion to include the whole of the top team. The relationship between chairmen and chief executives has become an issue in its own right in the debate on governance in Britain and is even being questioned in the United States, where the combination of the two top posts has long been taken for granted.

The Committee on the Financial Aspects of Corporate Governance emphasised, in its Report, the crucial part which chairmen play in securing good corporate governance and went on to say:

> Given the importance and particular nature of the chairman's role, it should in principle be separate from that of the chief executive. If the two roles are combined in one person, it represents a considerable concentration of power. *We recommend*, therefore, that there should be a clearly accepted division of responsibilities at the head of a company, which will ensure a balance of power and authority, such that no one individual has unfettered powers of decision. Where the chairman is also the chief executive, it is essential that there should be a strong and independent element on the board.

The Committee was fully aware that what mattered was the board structure in its entirety and not solely whether the two top posts were combined. One of the more vocal criticisms of the Committee's recommendations was, however, that it should have made their separation mandatory for listed companies. This may primarily reflect the lessons learnt by investors during a recession, but it also reveals a new and welcome interest in corporate governance. A sound corporate structure cannot of itself ensure commercial success, but one without appropriate checks and balances increases the risk of disaster. What are, therefore, the respective roles of chairmen and of chief executives and how do they fit together at the head of a business?

Leadership

Lord McFadzean, writing in 1972 in *International Management* on the key tasks of a company chairman, underlined the chairman's responsibility to instigate and to inspire policy. Both are aspects of the chairman's leadership role and it is for leadership that the board and the company are looking to the chairman in an increasingly uncertain world. What they want are chairmen with a sense of vision and a clear idea of the direction which they feel their company should take. That sense of vision includes not only the company's tangible objectives but also its character, the kind of company which it is and which it aims to become. Chairmen as instigators and inspirers assume a responsibility for the continuity of their businesses; in framing their company's goals they are looking to the enterprise of the future.

The most compelling description of the chairman's role, in this context, is summed up in Sir John Harvey-Jones's words – 'It is through the board that the company takes its drumbeat from the chairman.' That says all that needs to be said about leadership. The board as a whole is responsible for the company's forward march, but its pace and direction are set by the chairman.

Bid pressures

The importance of that strategic lead from the top, the chairman's drumbeat, remains unchanged. What are, however, continually changing are the challenges to the future of their companies which chairmen have to face. Today, even the largest companies and those with the best-defined strategies are open to bids of various kinds, which reflect remarkable financial ingenuity, not always equally matched by managerial logic. The ability to raise large amounts of debt on a narrow equity base has widened the opportunities for bidders to a degree which was unimaginable a relatively short time ago. It has provided a means of extracting the maximum immediate value from a company's assets and of substituting debt for equity on a grand scale.

The bid threat remains, even when the pace of takeover activity ebbs with the economic tide. Chairmen and their boards are, therefore, only too well aware that quoted companies may be bid targets at any time. The possibility of an offer for their company has not only given added emphasis to the leadership task of the chairman, but it has altered its nature as well. The chairman has to combine leading the company towards its future goals with being ready to defend its independence on possibly the most short-term of considerations.

Effect of these pressures on structure

The increased demands which may now be made of the chairman as leader are relevant to whether the post should or should not be combined with that of the chief executive. The argument for splitting them would be that if a company is under threat, there is advantage in having a chairman who can give all the time needed to masterminding the company's defence, while the chief executive concentrates on the ongoing task of running the company. Incidentally, this draws attention to one of the basic differences between the two roles: the chief executive's job is unremitting; the running of the business requires continual oversight, while the chairman's workload is more variable and is determined by the calls made on it. Given that companies can be under siege for some time (one of the hidden costs of the bid process), those that argue for the split say that the chief executive should always be in place to give the management lead which any enterprise demands under those circumstances.

The counter-argument is that in times of hazard it is essential that there should be no ambiguity about who is in charge of every aspect of the business and that the combined chairman and chief executive provides precisely that individual leadership which both the forward march and the defence of the company demand.

This is just one facet of the debate about the merits of separating or combining the roles of chairman and chief executive. In the meantime, before considering the arguments for and against those two options, it may be helpful to look more closely at practical ways in which chairmen and chief executives can work together. In discussing how, rather than whether, they should share the leadership, we have to bear in mind that one of the key factors in the division of responsibilities between them is how much time the chairman spends in the company.

THE DIVISION OF RESPONSIBILITY

The full-time chairman's role

The primary distinction is between full-time chairmen and those who only give part of their time to chairing a particular company. Full-time chairmen, whose main job is their chairmanship, can be expected to cover most of the range of internal and external responsibilities of the chairman which have already been discussed. They will be responsible for the leadership of the board and for all aspects of the board's work – that it has the right people on it and addresses itself to the right issues, and that it sets the course for the company and sees that this course is maintained. On the external side, they will normally be the public face of the company, with all that that entails, and accountable for its results to the outside world.

This represents a practical division of responsibilities between a chairman and a chief executive. The chairman sees that the board does its job and minds the company's external relationships, so protecting the chief executive from being distracted from the task of managing the company's operations. To oversimplify, the chairman could be said to look primarily outwards and the chief executive primarily inwards. The chairman is responsible for ensuring that the board makes the necessary decisions and the chief executive is responsible for carrying them out. In this split, all executive instructions would go out in the name of the chief executive and the only people who would report direct to chairmen would be their immediate support staff.

An alternative approach

Hugh Parker, in his *Letters to a New Chairman* (1990), outlines a somewhat different division of duties, which would tilt the balance rather more towards the chairman. This is in the context of a chairman who has just moved into the post after being the managing director, and who is now contemplating appointing a replacement managing director. Hugh Parker advises the chairman, when he makes the appointment, to stick to the established British title, 'group managing director', rather than to convert it into that of 'chief executive'. The titles of chairman and of managing director are explicit and line up broadly with the American division between a chairman/chief executive officer and a president/chief operating officer.

Unfortunately, titles in Britain do have a significance of their own, and in sizeable companies the description of chief executive has become well established, so Hugh Parker's new chairman will probably have to come into line. If he does, then that underlines the importance of his sticking with the straightforward and explicit title of chairman and not adding the label 'non-executive'. Whatever the split, the final responsibility for the company rests with the chairman and the designation which is given to the chief executive/managing director should not detract from the chairman's position.

Reporting relationships

If the division is along American lines, the managing director in Hugh Parker's example would report to the chairman. In the split which I outlined, the chief executive would be responsible to the board, for whom the chairman stands in between meetings, rather than directly to the chairman. On the question of what resources of their own chairmen might have, Hugh Parker has this advice to give:

> You will need some high-quality staff to back you up – e.g. to provide you with legal, financial, corporate planning, PR and perhaps other functional support – and therefore these corporate staff units should almost certainly report directly to you. And in addition, depending on how you and Jim Bennett decide to share and balance the total workload, the heads of some line operating units might also report to you, at least initially. (p. 63)

As chief executive or managing director, I would argue against heads of line operating units reporting to the chairman. It means that the source of executive instructions is divided, which can in turn lead to wires being crossed unintentionally or intentionally. It is particularly important, when managing directors become chairmen, that they should move as completely as possible out of their previous position, in order to give their successors a proper chance to establish themselves in their new post.

The chairman's authority

Chairmen have clear legal, financial and public relations responsibilities and the issue of whether the staff who support them in these fields report direct to them or not is a practical one, for the people concerned to decide. Nevertheless, it provides a useful peg on which to hang a comment on the nature of the chairman's authority. If they have legal, financial and PR staff for whom they are responsible, they have executive authority to ask them to carry out whatever tasks need to be done. If those staff do not report direct to them, they can still arrange to have the same work done, but would normally do so through the chief executive or the functional director concerned. The chairman's effective authority is the same in both situations, but in the first case it is exercised as the executive head of a function and in the second it is exercised on behalf of the board. The authority to get things done – to execute – is not dependent on having executive responsibility for people.

The other function which Hugh Parker mentions as being one for which a chairman might retain responsibility is corporate planning. This would line up naturally with the chairman's responsibility for the continuity of the business, but it is a field in which both the chairman and the chief executive need to be involved, a point to which we will return in the next chapter.

The need for clarity

The phrase with which the passage ends 'at least initially' underlines the protean nature of the relationship between a chairman and a chief executive. Newly appointed chief executives may well leave more to their chairmen than will seem appropriate as they gain experience. What is essential is that the split between them should be unequivocally clear when their partnership is established. As they work together, confidence is built between them and they sort out how best to complement each other. From there on their pattern of working can be adjusted more informally to meet the needs of the enterprise.

The outside chairman's role

When chairmen are only involved with a company for part of their time, there is no difference in principle between their role and that of a full-time chairman. They hold the same office and their chairman-ship is as all-embracing. This is why the title 'part-time chairman' is misleading. A more accurate description of their position within a company is the American one of 'outside chairman' and that is the title which I will use. The practical difference between these two types of chairmanship is the time which outside chairmen can give to their companies, or which their companies expect of them; this, in turn, will determine the way in which they divide their responsibilities with their chief executives.

In smaller companies

If, for example, a company has just moved from the stage of owner-management to that of enlisting outside investors, then the person managing the business may want an experienced independent chairman solely to chair board meetings and to act as the link with investors and the financial world. Such chairmen might be solicitors or accountants, who already hold some company chairmanships in addition to their professional work. They might need to spend relatively little time at the company's offices, but they would bring with them the knowledge which the managing director lacked and they would enable the managing director to get on with that which he or she knew best and did best – the running of the business.

In larger companies

At the other end of the scale, in large companies, outside chairmen might well spend half their time on the company's affairs. They would be as responsible for giving a lead to the company and for the work of the board as would a full-time chairman. Their ability to be responsible for external relationships would necessarily be more limited. The chief executive and other board members could be expected to take over some of what a full-time chairman might do in this respect.

For example, the work of keeping in touch with financial analysts, institutional investors and sources of finance might be divided between the chairman, the chief executive and the finance director. More appearances on behalf of the company might be made by the chief executive and, if the company had international activities, the chief executive and other members of the top team might undertake more of the overseas visits, which are such an essential aspect of holding a worldwide business together.

The precise division of duties between an outside chairman and a chief executive would depend, first, on the time the former made available to the company and, second, on the abilities and preferences of the two individuals.

ONE JOB OR TWO?

To return to the specific question of whether the chairman should also be chief executive, what are some of the arguments for separating the two posts and for combining them?

The chairman/chief executive

There are two general points to be made in support of the chairman being the chief executive as well. One is that, taking British companies as a whole, it remains the most favoured approach to defining the top job, although there has been a marked drop in the number of public companies which combine the roles in the last five years. In 1989, half of *The Times* top 1,000 companies designated their senior director as chairman and chief executive, by 1994 fewer than one quarter did so. However, it would be normal in a smaller company for whoever is running the enterprise to combine both roles. Given that there are roughly 1,500 times as many private as public companies in Britain, one person at the head of the business has to be the most common arrangement.

This runs on to the second point which is that most companies are founded by an individual, who is likely to be the owner and the manager. All being well, they remain in charge of their businesses as they grow, being responsible for their direction and their management. In that sense they are chairmen/chief executives. Then, a number of reasons can arise for wanting to differentiate between the two posts, such as the introduction of outside sources of finance, ownership and management becoming divorced, or the founder wishing to take more of a back seat.

Whatever the reason, dividing the responsibilities for heading a company means dividing a position which was originally a unity. This concept of unity at the top is of crucial importance in considering how the job can be divided, an issue which has already been discussed and to which we will return. At this stage, the point which is being registered is simply that the two top posts are naturally combined in one person in the formative stages of a company's development.

The need for leadership

When it comes to the argument for retaining the founder's position and combining the role of the chairman with that of the chief executive, it is, at its simplest, that the combination provides the company with the strongest possible leadership. There is no ambiguity about who is head of the company. For those in the company and for those outside it, who have a direct or indirect interest in its affairs, the source of authority is clear. One person is responsible for ensuring that the board frames the company's strategy and the policies which accompany it, and the same person is responsible for putting these into effect. The accountability of the chairman/chief executive is unequivocal.

To take a British example, this appears to have been the overriding argument when the board of Guinness appointed their chief executive as their chairman after the acquisition of the Distillers company in 1986. The board had originally agreed to appoint an independent chairman of the highest standing, once the acquisition had gone through, but then appear to have taken the view that only a unified command at the top of the combined company could achieve the targeted, post-acquisition results. The subsequent acceptance by the shareholders in general meeting of the board's decision not to appoint an independent chairman meant either that they were convinced by the argument that the necessary leadership could only be exercised by one person, or that they did not consider the matter important enough to demand their vote.

Reasons for combining the roles

The arguments, therefore, on the side of combining the roles of the chairman and of the chief executive are that it is common practice, that it is the way in which companies are run by their founders and that it provides undisputed leadership internally and externally.

Lastly, we are not simply discussing the narrow question of whether there should be one or two people at the head of an enterprise. Either way they are part of a board. Thus it is the way in which the board as a whole works, which sets the framework for those at its head. It is the counterbalance provided by the other board members which will determine whether or not the combination of the two posts confers an unacceptable degree of power on one person.

Chairman but not chief executive

The three main arguments for separating the roles of chairman and of chief executive are as follows: first, that different mixes of ability are required for the two posts; second, that putting the two positions together concentrates too much power in the hands of one person; and third, that the combination makes it more difficult for the board to carry out its supervisory function.

Difference in roles

On the first argument, the two posts call, I would suggest, for somewhat different qualities and strengths. Both the chairman and the chief executive need to have the capacity to lead, but leadership of the board and of the company externally is not the same as leading the managers and the work-force. Given that the board's job is to define the purpose of the company and how it is to be achieved, its chairman needs to have strategic sense, the ability to analyse the competitive environment and the capacity to stand back from the business of today.

There is an understandable difference in time horizons between the chairman, who has a responsibility for the long-term survival of the enterprise, and the chief executive, who appreciates that, unless this year's budget is delivered, there may be no long-term future for the chairman to consider. The chief executive, in carrying out the board's strategy, has above all to have the ability to make the right things happen. Of course, one person can be excellent both at strategy and at putting strategy into effect, as all successful commanders have been, but most of us are better at one than the other, or become better at one than the other.

Antony Jay, whose writings on management should be better known, draws a forceful distinction between the roles of the chairman and of the chief executive in his book, *Corporation Man* (p. 99):

> The difference is so profound that it is practically impossible to discharge both duties properly at the same time. The present and the future do not run in harness: their demands and emphases move at a different pace and sometimes pull in opposite directions, and it is rarely satisfactory if the conflict takes place in a single man's mind. If one man tries to do both jobs, one of them is likely to go by default.

The job which most probably will go by default is that of creating tomorrow's company out of today's. Separating the roles, therefore, provides a safeguard against the future being mortgaged to the present. It also presents an opportunity to appoint people with different strengths, and perhaps of different ages and backgrounds, to the top two posts, thereby spreading the workload between them and drawing on a wider range of attributes than would be possible with a single appointment. To reap the benefits of the split in this way, it is of course essential to make the appointments the right way round. To have the man of action as the chairman, and the strategist as the chief executive, will create problems down the line. Having said that, it is possible to have a chief executive who is primarily a strategist and who delegates much of the carrying-out of the strategy; but in that case they will need a chairman who accepts a matching role, which will be more limited than the one I have previously outlined.

Concentration of power

The second argument concerns the concentration of power and this must be addressed, because of the way in which companies are governed in practice rather than in theory. Shareholders, in the normal course of events, have little control over the actions of the board which they have appointed, or in whose appointment they have acquiesced. The safeguard on which they are relying is that the board keeps their interests in mind and monitors the management to that effect. This safeguard is, however, structurally weakened if the chairman of the board is also responsible as chief executive for the management of the business.

Checks and balances

The separation of the two roles builds in a check and a balance. Chairmen have a clear responsibility to ensure that their boards take account of the interests of the shareholders and that they carry out their supervisory functions conscientiously. Chairmen, who are also chief executives, have to be scrupulously clear in their own minds when they are acting as the one and when as the other, as they move between the two roles. It can be done and it is done, but it is less demanding on all concerned to divide the roles rather than the individual.

When someone who holds both positions is determined on a course of action, which perhaps entails high risks for the company, who is to challenge their judgement? Their executive directors are their subordinates away from the board meeting and so it falls to the outside directors on the board to question the possible consequences of what is being proposed. It is not always easy for those outside the business to do this rigorously, since chief executives have the staff resources of the company behind them in making their case, whether or not the staff share the doubts of the outsiders.

The power of the chairman added to the power of the chief executive presents a formidable combination. This is recognised by those who hold both posts. For example, in an article in the September 1989 issue of the *Director* magazine, Lord Blakenham, who was then chairman and chief executive of the Pearson group (he is now solely its chairman), is quoted as saying:

I believe being chairman and chief executive is not an ideal arrangement, although it suits the type of group we have. It is easier to justify if you have a strong board of outside directors than if you have two or three rather cosy directors. If you combine chairman with chief executive and do not have a strong board he becomes too powerful within the group. (Bose 1989)

Need for safeguards

That represents a balanced view of the whole question of whether or not the roles should be combined and focuses on the vital safeguards if they are: first, that chairmen should themselves be conscious that the arrangement is not ideal and, second, that the combination demands a strong board. The particular importance of the second safeguard is that it is the job of the board as a whole, not just that of the deputy chairman or of the outside directors on it, to ensure that the chairman/chief executive's power is harnessed for the good of the company.

But to put the argument at its bluntest, how do board members carry out their duty to monitor and, if necessary, to replace the chief executive, when the chief executive is also their chairman? There have been recent instances in Britain and in the United States of the chief executives of major companies being dismissed by their boards. They have occurred, most immediately, where there was an independent chairman, who was in a position to see that the board squared up to this most difficult of all decisions.

Where the action has had to be taken by the outside directors on their own, the process could be expected to be less clear-cut and more protracted. This has led to the proposal in the United States – and one already enacted at General Motors – that the outside directors should select a 'lead director' from among their number, to make up in part for the lack of a separate chairman. It is asking the impossible to expect chairmen/chief executives to apply equally objective standards as chairmen to their own management performance as chief executives.

Similar difficulties arise over succession. When the time comes for chairmen/chief executives to retire, the task of their replacement is more difficult to handle than the retirement of one or the other. Chairmen would normally take the lead over the appointment of the successor to the chief executive, and one of their responsibilities is to see that there are potential successors.

Equally, it is for the board, and particularly for the outside members of the board, to arrange for the chairman's succession. Chairmen/chief executives are in a position to have a major say in their own departure and over who should succeed them. This may not result either in a timely retirement or in a satisfactory handover. It is significant that Harold Geneen, who was highly successful in building up ITT, but had little time for boards of directors, should have failed so conspicuously in the matter of his own succession. This comes out clearly in Robert Schoenberg's book on Geneen's remarkable career. He dominated ITT for twenty years and increased its sales nearly thirty times to make it a major international company. But his business empire fell apart when he retired too late, having failed to bring on a successor.

The conclusion is clear. There has to be someone on the board who is in a position to tell chairmen/chief executives when the time has come for them to go, and to make sure, in the meantime, that responsibility is being handed on to potential successors. If there is no such person on the board, then the posts need to be split.

The board has to act as a board

The third argument is in a sense an extension of the same point. It is that chairmen, whose primary responsibility is ensuring that the board works as it should, will find it easier to discharge this responsibility in full than chairmen/chief executives. For chairmen/ chief executives this is only part of their job and not the part on which their performance will be judged outside the board. What is at stake is not solely the board's supervisory role – the single head having the responsibility as chairman of monitoring their own actions as chief executive – though that is an important element in the argument and one which should concern shareholders. It also applies to the board's initiatory role, to its constructive questioning of policies and plans and its contribution to strategic thinking.

The board is a deliberative body and its deliberations take a different shape from those of a management committee. As has already been discussed, its members have equal duties and responsibilities and it is for chairmen to see that board members, executive and outside directors alike, participate in board debates on equal terms with their colleagues. When the relationship between the board members and the chairman is only through the board, then executive directors are clear that they are not in a management forum and that they are expected to act as full directors of the company. If the chief executive is in the chair, then both the chief executive and the executive directors have to be conscious that their relationship has changed; at the board meeting the chief executive is no longer their executive head, but a chairman among equals.

In addition, the course of discussion at the board is not the same as it would be in a management committee. The management proposals which come to the board have probably been thrashed out at an executive committee chaired by the chief executive. If the chief executive is then in the chair at the board, it requires a deliberate effort on their part not to have a re-run of the executive committee discussion. The chief executive could also be forgiven for feeling that all the critical points had already been argued out and that the board discussion should therefore be kept as brief as it decently could be.

If, on the other hand, the chief executive and the executives on the board have to present their proposals to a chairman and to outside directors, who were not party to the discussions leading up to the presentation, their approach will not be the same as it was to their fellow-managers. They will be putting their proposals to informed outsiders and will need to think through how their ideas and plans will look to competent colleagues, who do not automatically share the same assumptions. This is likely to add a useful dimension to the proposals themselves and to the grounds for advancing them, quite apart from any modifications to them or new lines of thinking about them, which may arise from the board debate.

The chairman as arbiter

The last point to be made on the advantages of dividing the two posts is that the division enables the chairman to act as an arbiter, when the need arises. Since chairmen would not normally be involved in the kind of executive decisions which might give rise to appeals, they are in a position to come to a judgement on them. This may avoid having to settle such issues outside the company and, well handled by chairmen, their resolution will enhance the company's reputation in the eyes of the complainants. I would not rate this as an argument for the separation of powers at the head of a company, but it illustrates that there are advantages to be gained from having a chairman who is independent of the executive.

Conclusions

Separation of the posts

I am in favour of separating the posts of chairman and chief executive or managing director, wherever it is feasible to do so. The small company which has just brought in outside investors can benefit from having an outside chairman, who may spend relatively little time in the company, but who chairs the board and takes responsibility for the company's external relationships, while the managing director concentrates entirely on the running of the business. In large companies, there is more than enough work to be done at the top for it to be usefully spread between chairmen, chief executives, deputy chairmen and finance directors.

The arguments which convince me from my experience that the chairman should not also be the chief executive are that the two jobs call for a different mix of abilities and perhaps of temperaments, that combined they represent too great a concentration of power and that it is easier to ensure that the board works as it should when they are divided. I also believe that chairmanship is a more demanding and specialised role than is generally appreciated.

I accept that people are more important than structures, so that the right people can make most organisational patterns work. But this is not to say that structures are unimportant. The objective should be to design structures which make it as easy as possible for office-holders to do what is expected of them. Combining the two posts requires chairmen/chief executives to continually remember which of the two hats they are wearing, or ought to be wearing. Why land an individual with that problem of self-identification, when it can be avoided by giving both the chairman and the chief executive separate responsibilities, so minimising the likelihood of conflicts of interest?

The argument that, in the United States, the CEO is usually the chairman as well does not alter my conclusion. In the first place, it could be said to fit with the American political and social pattern, in the same way that the United States has an executive President, while Britain has a Prime Minister who chairs a Cabinet. Second, the make-up of American boards is different from that of British boards and the CEO may be the only executive member of a US board. This means that the problem of chairing a board of equals, some of whom are your executive subordinates, is less likely to arise.

Having said that, I believe that CEO/chairmen run boards, and probably select boards, differently from the way in which chairmen whose sole task is chairing the board would do. Hugh Parker, in an interesting article in *Directors and Boards* (Spring 1994) on the arguments for considering the separation of the two top posts in the United States, mentions that CEOs have been known to refer to their boards as if they were another department which needed to be 'managed'. Although that may be an extreme position, CEO/ chairmen could be said to look to their boards to back their plans and policies, while chairmen as such look to their boards to formulate plans and policies.

What determines the split?

How should the separation of responsibilities be arrived at? The precise division will turn on the abilities and inclinations of the people concerned and on the time that the chairman spends in the company. Then there are such practical considerations to be taken into account as which of them was in place first.

The natural split, in my view, is that the chairman is in charge of the board and all its works, while the chief executive is responsible for everything outside the board. Under this division, all management instructions are issued by the chief executive, so that there is no doubt within the company as to who is in charge managerially. The chairman is nevertheless ultimately accountable for the company's actions and so has a right to be consulted and to be kept informed by the chief executive. The chairman carries the authority of the board, while the chief executive is specifically given executive authority by the board to put its decisions into effect.

I find this particular division of duties logical, because it is the one to which I have worked in the past. Variations on it are equally workable, given two conditions. First, that the chairman and the chief executive see their jobs as complementary and not as competing. Each is responsible for a part of what could be one job, so they have to ensure that their responsibilities match to make up a coherent whole. It is their ability to combine together to form an effective partnership at the head of the company which is crucial. Any whiff of competition between the chairman and the chief executive undermines the foundation of their relationship and will cause confusion down the line. This leads on to the second condition which is that the two individuals have to trust one another.

Need for definition

It is important that the split between the chairman and the chief executive should be defined by them and agreed with the board. It may well be necessary to re-define the division of duties between them as and when their relationship changes. It is equally important that the way in which they define their roles should be understood within the company and outside it.

Separation but not mandatory

Although I advocate separating the chairmanship from the post of chief executive in publicly quoted companies, I would not attempt to enforce that view statutorily. In the first place, I do not believe that the infinite variety of chairmen, chief executives, companies and circumstances can be strait-jacketed into one compulsory pattern of organisation. There are exceptional individuals who can achieve more for their companies holding both of the top positions, rather than sharing them. Equally, there can be stages in a company's development which could call for a single head.

Second, making a particular division of duties mandatory is not necessarily the best way of achieving the objectives of getting the most out of the board system and of providing a check on the power of an individual. It has been said, of organisation charts, that the interesting parts are the white spaces between the boxes, because that is where the real action takes place. Just as any organisational structure can be made to work by the right people, it follows that any structure can be bent to the purposes of those who are determined to do so.

The Committee's view

The Committee on the Financial Aspects of Corporate Governance did not specifically require the posts of chairman and of chief executive to be separated, although they made it clear in their Report, as opposed to in the Code of Best Practice, that in principle they should be. The Committee reasoned that every company was different and that each had to find the system of checks and balances which best suited its particular circumstances. Added to which, it would be contrary to observed experience to claim that combining the two roles could never work successfully.

The Committee also recognised that there was more to the governance structure than the posts of the chairman and of the chief executive alone. What matters is the quality of the board and also that the board structure, taken as a whole, should contain checks and balances which the shareholders consider adequate.

The Committee's Code of Best Practice, as we have seen, called for a clearly accepted division of responsibilities at the head of a company to ensure a balance of power and authority. It went on to say that where the chairman was also the chief executive, it was essential that there should be a strong and independent element on the board, with a recognised senior member.

The Committee, therefore, set out the tests which the governance structure of companies should meet, leaving boards to find ways of meeting them which were acceptable to their shareholders. Passing the tests set by the Code is a better guarantee of a genuine separation of powers at the head of a company, than simply having to give two board members different titles. It also provides shareholders with more of an opportunity to satisfy themselves as to the true balance of power within a company, than if the only point at issue was whether the two posts were separate or combined.

The aim is an effective board

Rather than laying down how the apex of the company's organisation chart should look on paper, the emphasis should be on the aim which lies behind the arguments for dividing the top job. The aim is to ensure that as many companies as possible are directed by effective and accountable boards. An effective board is one which gives the company the leadership it needs and in which the responsibilities for directing the enterprise are shared, so that the company is not overly dependent on one person. Accountability is safeguarded by building an acceptable system of checks and balances into the board structure.

The responsibility for making certain that companies are headed by effective boards lies squarely with the shareholders. The issue which is of prime concern to the institutions in particular, is whether the boards of the companies in which they have invested are competently led and have the appropriate mix of people on them. Provided the emphasis is on the end result – an effective board – then it should be accepted that the means to that end may vary. But shareholders should make it clear that separation is the rule and combination the exception. If a board claims that there is a need to combine the two top posts for a time, the shareholders should persist in asking the board when they expect to end what has already been categorised as a less than ideal arrangement.

Why are the top posts combined?

This brings us to the crucial question. If structural logic points to the separation of the roles of the chairman and of the chief executive, especially in larger companies and in public limited companies, why are the posts nevertheless combined as often as they are? The only answers which I can put forward are that finding the right match of people and personalities at the top is difficult and that there is a shortage of what might be called qualified chairmen.

The right match

On finding the right combination of people to share the top job, we need to keep in mind that either the chairman or the chief executive is likely to be already in place. If it is the chief executive who is in post, then the board has to find a new chairman with all the qualities which they are looking for in a chairman. In addition, potential candidates will have to be willing to accept whatever pattern of responsibilities will fit with those at present carried by the chief executive and be prepared to work harmoniously with whoever is in that seat. Given the limitations of the search process, this may seem a tall order and it is not surprising that some boards will decide that the course of least risk is to give the chairman's job to the chief executive.

Chairmen in short supply

When I refer to a lack of qualified chairmen, I mean that there are not enough people who see their abilities as lying primarily in the field of chairmanship and who wish to apply themselves to acquiring the skills which that role demands. Most chief executives would no doubt prefer to have a chairman with whom to share their responsibilities and with whom to talk issues through, provided that they could find someone whom they respected and from whom they felt they could learn.

One of the reasons why the combination does not always work out well is that there can be a gap in outlook between the new generation of chief executives and an older generation of chairmen. The focus of the new generation of chief executives is on performance and on winning in a commercial world which is considerably more competitive and more hostile than it probably was in their chairman's younger days. Unless such chief executives are matched by chairmen who can assist them in achieving their goals, chairmen will too often be seen as a brake on progress.

The way forward

I believe that the way forward is for companies (and indeed for non-profit-making institutions as well) to recognise the importance of the chairman's role and to appreciate that it requires certain skills. This would encourage those with the necessary bent to acquire the appropriate skills and to concentrate on chairmanship as a calling. They would then be in a position to offer their services as outside chairmen, on a part-time basis, to more than one company or body.

The move towards chairmanship as a part-time occupation would spread the benefits of experienced chairmanship, and I suspect that it would make it easier to match a chief executive with an appropriate chairman. An outside chairman can carry out the essential task of chairmanship – responsibility for the board – without taking on duties which might otherwise be done by the chief executive or members of the executive team.

A split of, say, one-third to two-thirds in terms of time between the chairman and the chief executive is probably an easier balance to work to in practice, than dividing the top job in half between two full-time people. The danger of complementarity edging into competition would thus be considerably reduced. I see the combination of experienced outside chairmen and full-time chief executives as being the most practical way of making the most of scarce skills and of giving the top partnership the best chance of succeeding.

CHAPTER 7

THE CHAIRMAN AND THE TOP TEAM

The main job of team-building lies with the chairman.
Clutterbuck and Waine

The previous chapter focused on the relationship between the post of the chairman and that of the chief executive. While this is the key relationship at board level, chairmen work with and through their other board colleagues. Their links with other members of the top team are, therefore, important, starting with their deputies.

DEPUTIES

The deputy chairman

In large companies there may be more than one deputy chairman, but for simplicity I will refer to the deputy chairmanship as a single post. There is a significant difference between the appellation of vice-chairman, which is a courtesy title, and that of deputy chairman. The deputy chairman stands in for the chairman and the potential importance of the deputy chairman's role seems to have been overlooked in the literature on boards. I regard the deputy chairman as being in a position to play a leading part in the top team, whether the chairman and the chief executive are one and the same person, or two people. I am primarily thinking here of companies of a size such that there is more than enough for the chairman and the chief executive to do on their own. If there is both a chairman and a chief executive, then the deputy chairman completes the triumvirate which constitutes the team at the top.

The deputy chairman's responsibilities

As full members of the top team, deputy chairmen share the work which falls to the head of the company. Provided that deputy chairmen are party to the thinking of their chairmen and their chief executives, they can represent the company's views externally or when visiting units within their companies. Like chairmen they speak for the board on such occasions.

Second, bringing the deputy chairman into the top team provides an opportunity to complement the abilities and experience of the chairman and the chief executive. I have worked as chairman with two different chief executives and, in each case, we had the good fortune to be supported by a wise and trusted deputy chairman. Both of these deputy chairmen brought additional attributes to the top team, given that they had broad business experience and a professional knowledge of the law and of finance, respectively. They were both outside directors, whereas I and the two chief executives concerned had spent our working lives in the business; thus they brought objectivity and independence of mind to our discussions. Both also undertook specific assignments on behalf of the board.

This leads on to a third point, which is that there are considerable advantages in discussing potentially divisive issues between three people rather than two. If a matter has to be resolved, two people can find themselves at odds and the only solution is for one to give way to the other. This is a normal feature of coming to decisions, but it puts a strain on the relationship between the two people involved. The win/lose situation can often be avoided if a third person, in whose impartial judgement the other two have complete confidence, is party to the discussions. In our case, we had the added advantage that both deputy chairmen, as outside directors, stood further back from the activities of the business than the chairman and the chief executive.

The deputy chairman, therefore, shares the burdens of the chairman's office and, ideally, should complement the chairman and the chief executive as well. The example I have given of the deputy chairman being an outside director, when the other two directors are insiders, could be reversed with an outside chairman; it might then be helpful to have an insider as deputy chairman. Either way, as much thought should be put into the appointment of a deputy chairman as into any other top appointment. At the same time it should be made clear that the post carries no pretensions to the chairmanship.

The relationship with the chairman/chief executive

The role of the deputy chairman becomes particularly significant when the chairman is also chief executive. The deputy chairman backed by the authority of the board is the counterbalance to the person who both chairs the board and manages the business. There is a good case for appointing an experienced outside director as deputy chairman under these circumstances. Again, the top team could become a triumvirate, if the chairman/chief executive appoints a deputy chief executive, in addition to the board appointing a deputy chairman. Power and authority would, however, be distributed differently in this case, since the deputy chief executive would be the chief executive's subordinate.

Triumvirates

A different triumvirate might be one made up of the chairman, the chief executive and the finance director. It is not quite the triangle of equals that it is when the deputy chairman is the third member, because the finance director would normally report to the chief executive. Nevertheless, the finance director's relationship with the chairman and with the chief executive is not the same as that of the other executive directors. Finance directors have a certain independence of position on the board and a direct line, whatever the reporting arrangements, to the other two. In many companies this is the effective top team.

I should perhaps make it clear that, when I refer to a triumvirate, I have in mind three people each with their own clearly defined post, but working together as a team at the head of a company. Another approach is to form an 'office of the chairman', as some large companies have done, and to focus attention on the group at the top, rather than on the individuals concerned and the division of responsibilities between them. I have no personal experience of this method of heading a company and it is such an unusual model that I will do no more than note its existence. It demonstrates that there is still enough dissatisfaction with traditional structures to encourage innovatory approaches to the task of company direction.

Clarity of purpose

In the end, those at the top of a company have certain duties to discharge and there are an endless number of ways in which those duties can be divided. The posts of chairman, deputy chairman and chief executive can be held by three people, or in different combinations by two people. The objectives remain the same: to provide clear leadership, to ensure that the board is effective and the business efficiently managed, and to represent the company to the outside world. The aim is to see that as many as possible of the qualities required for these different tasks are present among the members of the top team. How the tasks are allocated is less crucial than that there should be trust between the members of the team and no confusion about who does what.

THE CHAIRMAN'S OTHER BOARD LINKS

Clearly, chairmen need to have a wider range of contacts than solely with their chief executives or their deputy chairmen if they are to be as in touch with the state of their companies as their responsibilities demand. For example, chairmen are concerned with the continuity of their companies and so with the resources of people in them. This gives them a link with the personnel director, who will probably also provide professional advice on board salaries. There should be no objection to chairmen having direct contact with any executive director, provided that it is in furtherance of their board duties and provided that their lines of communication have been cleared with their chief executives. There are, however, two executives who would normally report to the chief executive, but who have particularly close ties with the chairman. They are the company or board secretary and the finance director.

The company secretary

At the chairman's right hand at board meetings is the company secretary. Company secretaries are responsible for board administration, whether or not they are full members of the board. Professional company secretaries who anticipate problems and who draft well make life a great deal easier for their chairmen. They prepare the board agenda with their chairmen, see that the right papers go out to board members on time and make certain that the necessary internal and external communications from the board are issued in the chairman's name – all other communications will be sent out under the authority of the chief executive.

It is standard practice for the company secretary to administer, attend and prepare minutes of board proceedings – drafting minutes is an art in itself. Sir Walter Puckey comments that, 'A board which arrives at the finishing post too late is a secretarial failure' (Puckey 1969, p. 187). I think that to hold board secretaries responsible for the length of either the meeting or the agenda is to load them with responsibilities which they do not have the authority to discharge. It is the chairman's fault if the meeting fails to reach the finishing post on time, and it is one which a competent board secretary will help chairmen to avoid.

The other main project on which the chairman and the company secretary are likely to work together is the company's annual report and accounts. Preparation of the report has to begin well before the year has ended and the company secretary is the logical person to lead the team which, in a company of any size, is responsible for the production of this important document. In spite of the fact that so many copies of the report and accounts are scarcely glanced at, it is the one regular direct communication from chairmen to their shareholders and it is kept by financial analysts and commentators as a source of information on the company. It is worth all the effort that goes into its preparation, and the company secretary can take much of the work involved off the chairman's shoulders.

The company secretary has a key role to play in ensuring that board procedures are followed and regularly reviewed. Chairmen will look to company secretaries for guidance on their legal responsibilities and duties. The company secretary should be in a position to give objective professional advice to the chairman and to other members of the board. Arguably, company secretaries are better placed to give this kind of impartial guidance if they are not themselves board members.

Chairmen will also be in close touch with their company secretaries over the range of regulations and official demands for information which apply, to a varying extent, to companies of all sizes. For quoted companies, there are stock exchange rules to be complied with and such matters as the rules governing notifications to shareholders and transactions in shares by directors. In addition to meeting the legal requirements of their home country, British companies have increasingly to be concerned with European regulations and with those of other countries in which they may have subsidiaries. In handling all the legal complexities which affect companies, board secretaries are the chairman's and the company's first line of defence. In drafting the board minutes, they ensure that they record the board's decisions, but offer no hostages to fortune should they be called in evidence by any of the regulatory authorities.

It follows on from the company secretary's responsibility for the report and accounts, that they would normally make the arrangements for the AGM. I always found it useful to go through with the company secretary all the eventualities which could arise at the AGM and he briefed me beforehand on possible shareholder questions which fell within his domain. The company secretary often acts as a link with shareholders and deals with shareholder correspondence which does not require the chairman's personal attention. In an increasingly regulated and litigious world, a legal rather than an accountancy training, combined with professional secretarial qualifications, has become the preferred background for a company secretary.

The finance director

The finance director stands in a special relationship to the chairman and to the chief executive, which is why the three of them often form the top team in a company. The basis of this relationship is the finance director's professional independence. It is the duty of finance directors to give their chairmen, chief executives and boards their own best judgement on the company's financial position. They are relied upon to present an unvarnished picture of the prospects for the company's half-year and full-year results, and where the risks to those prospects lie. Their relationship to their chief executives is more that of a professional adviser than that of an executive subordinate. They may well give their boards a more cautious view of the financial state of the business than their chief executives; what their chairmen and boards want to know is that they are capable of coming to their own informed judgement and sticking to it.

Chairmen are responsible for reporting their company's results publicly and so need to keep in close touch with their finance directors, and to have a feel for the way in which the figures are coming through. They have to know how to set their face in answer to questions from analysts, commentators and shareholders and in doing so they rely on the finance director for guidance as to the financial state of the business.

There are also decisions on matters like rights issues, borrowing limits and dividend payments which involve chairmen, but on which they will look to their finance directors for a lead. They will turn to them, too, in defending their companies against unwanted approaches from outside. Most companies which could be under threat of a hostile bid have an internal group in readiness, which is continually updating their defence strategy. The finance director will probably chair this group and act as the link with the company's professional advisers.

Finance directors may, with chief executives, be the main points of contact with the financial world, but, in giving a company view, finance directors are representing their chairmen and boards and so they and their chairmen have to be in close touch and in complete agreement as to how the company's financial position should be presented externally.

The auditors

The external auditors are not part of the company team, but chairmen have a direct interest in assuring themselves of the effectiveness of the audit approach within their companies. No chairman appreciates surprises, least of all in financial matters. Favourable surprises may be immediately welcome, but they raise doubts about the reliability of the information and control systems. Chairmen look first to their audit committees to ensure that the right relationship has been established between management and the external and internal auditors.

The auditors are formally appointed by the shareholders, although in practice selected by the company. It is the say in the choice of auditors which companies have, in reality, that makes the relationship between auditors and managers so crucial. The relationship should be one where the auditors work with the appropriate people in the company, but do so on a strictly objective and professional basis, never losing sight of the fact that they are there on the shareholders' behalf. Chairmen need auditors who will stand up to management when necessary and who will unhesitatingly raise any doubts about people or procedures with the audit committee or with themselves. Weak auditors expose chairmen to hazards.

A further reassurance for chairmen is for the external audit to be backed by an effective internal audit function. Internal auditors are in a position to monitor key controls and procedures regularly, to check on the efficiency with which they are being operated and to undertake investigations on behalf of the audit committee. Heads of internal audit should have unrestricted access to their audit committee chairmen to buttress the independence of their post.

The outside directors

The last set of relationships to consider are those between chairmen and the outside members of their boards. The chairman's position is an exposed and at times lonely one. Chairmen depend on their outside directors for advice, support and criticism. It is a great help to chairmen to be able to meet with the outside directors from time to time, with or without the chief executive. These meetings may be informal, but they give the chairman the chance to try out ideas, to share concerns and to discuss emerging issues before they have taken sufficient shape to be debated more widely.

Then there are matters concerning the top executives of the company, which chairmen can only discuss with their outside colleagues. It is because of the importance of this relationship between the chairman and the outside directors that such care has to be taken in adding to their number. The chairman has to be sure that any newcomers will strengthen the team of outside directors before their names are put forward.

The chairman has, of course, to avoid splitting the board between the outsiders and the insiders. However, the contributions of these two parts of the board are different and there is advantage in drawing on them separately at times. In the same way, chief executives usually meet with their executive directors in management committees which they chair. Chairmen need to make the most of all the counsel which their board colleagues have to offer, and there is no reason why the manner in which they consult them should impair the unity of the board.

THE CHAIRMAN'S RESPONSIBILITY FOR STRATEGY

Finally, there is the question of the chairman's responsibility for the strategy of the company. It is dealt with here, because it is an aspect of the division of duties between chairmen and their chief executives, and because the formulation of strategy involves chairmen and all their board colleagues.

It is a key issue because, on the whole, successful strategies are those which are consistently pursued. The quality of a strategy is clearly important, but less so, in my view, than its continuity and the commitment with which it is driven home. All of which means that the chairman and the chief executive have to be at one over the course they set for the company.

Both the chairman and the chief executive have a responsibility to ensure that the company is working to a strategy which is understood inside the company and externally. Establishing a strategy is an issue over which they collaborate; it is not the separate responsibility of one or other of them. Strategy is a classic board responsibility and it is, therefore, in the chairman's field. Equally, the chairman is responsible for seeing that the company has an identifiable sense of purpose and that this purpose is regularly reviewed, in order to ensure the company's continuity in a turbulent competitive environment. In addition, the chairman is likely to have the task of putting across the company's aims to outside audiences. For all these reasons, the chairman needs to be involved in the development of the strategy of the enterprise.

Strategic options

Chief executives in their turn will be responsible for preparing the strategic options and for putting them to the board. Since they will be in charge of carrying out the agreed strategy, it has to be one to which, in its final shape, they are committed personally and absolutely. Hammering out a strategy is an iterative process in which ideas and plans move backwards and forwards between the board and the various levels of management. It is a process which has to be approached from the bottom up, as well as from the top down.

The board sets the boundaries within which operating units draw up their individual forward plans. In doing so, the operating units can be expected to put forward proposals which build on their existing activities. It is for the board, however, to take an overall view of the future shape of the company and to decide which of the existing activities should be developed and which should not. It is the synthesis of these two views of the company that the chief executive will put to the board – a synthesis which may only be arrived at after considerable internal discussion.

Strategic proposals

The strategic proposals which come to the board will represent the considered judgement of those within the company as to the direction which the business should be taking. These proposals then have to be reviewed by the board as a whole, where the outside directors will see them through different eyes, since they are outside the company looking in. In practice, it is far from easy to involve all board members usefully in a discussion of strategy and it may be best to do so separately from a regular board meeting. It requires imaginative effort, by both the chairman and the chief executive, to present strategic issues to board members early enough in the process for them to have real influence over the outcome, and in a form which encourages them to contribute positively to the development of the final strategy.

Strategic continuity

Chairmen have a particular part to play in stimulating their boards to reflect creatively on the company's strategy. They have the advantage over their chief executives in that they have handed over the responsibility for achieving the current year's results, and so are free to concentrate their thinking on the years ahead. This is not meant to imply that the chief executive should be responsible for short-term results and the chairman for longer-term objectives. The development of a company is a continuous process and cannot be broken up into annual increments. The chairman and the chief executive have, therefore, to work together to make certain that the actions taken in the company today are in line with their plans for the company of tomorrow.

CHAPTER 8

REPRESENTING THE COMPANY

Election of the chairman is the responsibility of the board; the whole tone of the company and its public image must be set by the board and, in particular, by positive leadership by the chairman. No company can be successful unless the chairman is of a calibre to provide this leadership and to represent the company properly to the outside world.

CBI Watkinson Report

THE CHAIRMAN'S REPRESENTATIONAL ROLE

The Watkinson Report

In 1973, the Confederation of British Industry's Company Affairs Committee under the chairmanship of Lord Watkinson published its report on the responsibilities of the British public company. Although addressed to public companies, its guidance is equally relevant to private companies. The Report is an important document in its own right and has influenced the direction of company legalisation since it was published. It was drawn up by business leaders and sets out their collective view of what is now expected of boards and of their chairmen. The Report described for the first time what companies in practice saw as their obligations, as opposed to those which an out-of-date and out-of-touch legal framework prescribed.

One of the points which comes clearly through in the Report is the significance of the chairman's role. The Report marks the acceptance of the transition of the chairman, from chairman of the board to chairman of the company. In addition, the extract from the Report which heads this chapter emphasises that it is the job of the chairman to provide leadership and to represent the company properly to the outside world.

It also sets in context the chairman's representational role. The board members share the responsibility for the public image of the company and for electing the chairman to represent them and the company. As always, the degree to which this responsibility for the company's external relations will be discharged by the chairman personally will vary between chairmen and between companies. The responsibility, however, rests firmly with chairmen, irrespective of the size of the company and of the way in which they delegate their duties in this regard. There will also be occasions when companies are faced with crises or issues of great moment, and it is the chairman who will be expected at these times to respond on behalf of the board.

Defining the audience

The chairman's representational role has become more onerous as the number of outside bodies with an interest in the activities of companies has grown. The key question for chairmen is to whom precisely are they representing their companies on any particular occasion. The more clearly they can define their audience, the more certain they can be that their message to them will be relevant in its content and appropriate in its form. Chairmen also have to consider the degree of control which they have over what goes out in their or their companies' name. What appears in the company report is under their control; what appears in an edited interview is not. This is one of the reasons why company reports are worth a considerable investment of time and thought by chairmen and their teams.

Openness

The chairman's overall aim in representing the company publicly is to ensure that the outside world is as well informed as possible about the company and that it sees its activities in a positive light. I believe that it is both right and sensible for chairmen to be as open as they prudently can be about the affairs of their companies. Openness minimises the risk of commentators being caught unawares by changes in the company's fortunes, which inevitably damages confidence in the competence of those running it. Openness also builds goodwill towards the company which can be drawn on in times of difficulty. Lastly, the more information which is openly available about a company, the less chance there is of anyone gaining a financial advantage through privileged knowledge.

The task of chairmen in representing their companies can be discussed under three main headings: their relationship with the shareholders, with the financial institutions, including the institutions as shareholders, and with the media.

The shareholder audience

Representing the company to the shareholders is a good illustration of the need to define the audience. Shareholders can be divided into two distinct groups from the outset – private individuals and institutions. In 1988, 88 per cent of Cadbury Schweppes' shareholders were private persons; between them they held 15.6 per cent of the shares. This understates the number of individual shareholders, since some hold their shares for convenience in nominee holdings, although as a result they will not receive communications direct from the company.

Banks, nominees, pension funds and insurance and investment companies, on the other hand, held 81 per cent of the shares and accounted for 11 per cent of the shareholders. The information requirements of these two groups are clearly different, although there will be differences within those categories as well, between active and passive shareholders, for example, and between those who look principally to the company for information and those who rely more on outside advice.

There are two other shareholder audiences, which chairmen also need to keep in mind. Employee shareholders are one, and they are becoming an increasingly important group in most companies. They are interested along with the other shareholders in the profitability of the business as a whole, but they also have a particular interest in the activities of the part of the company to which they belong. In meeting their special interests, care has to be taken that they do not receive significantly more information than is generally made available to shareholders.

The second audience is that of potential shareholders. Companies benefit from having as wide a spread of shareholders as possible, both geographically and as between types of shareholder. In framing their messages to present shareholders, chairmen will also be aiming to reach those institutions and individuals who might become shareholders in the future.

The chairman's main line of communication with the shareholders is the full report which is sent to them annually and the much shorter report which goes out at the half-year.

The company report

The annual report has to meet a number of needs and to address a number of audiences. The skill in preparing it lies in the degree to which these different aims can be reconciled, while still coming out with a document which is coherent and conveys some flavour of the company. In Britain, the annual report and the accounts which accompany it have to meet both legal and accounting requirements and those of the London Stock Exchange (if the company is listed) and of other regulatory bodies. From time to time it has further special charges laid upon it, such as to report on the steps which the company is taking to encourage employee involvement, to comply with the Code of Best Practice on corporate governance and to care for the environment.

The bucket

The list grows longer as new issues attract attention, and these various demands for information are largely unrelated to each other. In the words of a Cooper & Lybrand report published in 1978, it has become essential 'to prevent the annual report from becoming the bucket into which different types of information are collated'. The dilemma for the chairman, with whose statement the annual report opens, is how to balance the continuing demand for more information with the need to keep the report readable and intelligible, at least in parts.

Into the bucket has to go everything the outside authorities demand and everything the company believes could be of interest to the shareholders, and to those who consult the annual report as a work of reference. What differentiates the annual report from other company communications is that it is of lasting value, and it will be kept by analysts and the media as a continuing source of information about the company. The report also has its place as a marketing document. Nevertheless, from the point of view of the majority of shareholders, the annual report has become unnecessarily long, complicated and costly.

The needs of shareholders

In my 1976 statement to the shareholders of Cadbury Schweppes, I referred to my concern over the increasing complexity of the annual report and I contrasted it with the report on the events of the year published by the company for its employees. In effect, the company was producing two annual reports. The content of the employee report was determined by its readership, while much of the content of the shareholders' report was determined by outside agencies. The logical next step seemed to me to be for companies to send the full report to those who wanted it, especially to those who wanted it for the record, and a shorter, more relevant version to everyone else. I finished by saying the following:

> There is a strong case for starting with what it is shareholders would like to know about their company and limiting the words and figures they are sent to those which meet that need; the fully annotated accounts could then be provided to anyone who required them. It would be interesting to know how many of the 42 pages in this document the majority of shareholders feel are superfluous.

I received a stimulating response from a number of those shareholders, who had struggled through to page four of the report where the question was posed. Their answers were mainly curt and to the point. What they wanted were the salient facts on the business as a whole, why the figures were better or worse than expected and what the outlook was for the future. They found three-quarters of the report irrelevant, including most of the figures, but encouragingly they asked for more information on the company's product range.

This showed that the shareholders took a practical interest in the company's activities, but their interest was less in what the company owned and earned, than in what it made and marketed. While I accept that this interest was in part prompted by the nature of the company, I suspect that most shareholders would react in much the same way, regardless of whether their company manufactured consumer products or not.

The simplified option

I believe that it would be in everyone's interests if shareholders could choose to receive either the whole bucketful or an edited version, which focused on those matters in which they had expressed an interest. An enquiry undertaken by the Institute of Chartered Accountants in 1978 showed that over half of all private shareholders would welcome a simplified annual report. Support for this option will grow in the European Union, if the movement towards harmonisation lengthens the list of items which have to be included in the full report. This will be particularly so if the European Commission decides that all employees should be sent copies of the annual report. No doubt the Green Party will campaign for a shortened version as well on sound ecological grounds.

Readable reports

In the meantime, the general standard of annual reports has improved, as more companies have employed professional design teams and as the techniques of printing and of presentation have advanced. There are a number of ways in which chairmen can make the most of their annual reports and accounts, in spite of the financial and legal barnacles with which they are encumbered.

The first is to ensure that a single hand edits the publication from start to finish, so that the report has coherence and continuity. Second, it is essential that the words and figures should be consistent throughout and that they should tell the same story. Putting current costs alongside historical costs transgressed that rule and led to confusion. If one set of figures was certified as 'true and fair', was the other set somehow truer and fairer, or just different?

This leads on to the third point, which is that the professionals have to be reminded that the purpose of the accounts and of the rules which lie behind them is to convey useful information to the shareholders. A minor illustration of where accounting jargon impedes understanding is in the officially required use of the word 'turnover' for sales. In North America, a turnover is something you eat – as in apple turnover – and the reports of British companies are not just addressed to shareholders in this country. In any case, even the accounting definition of 'turnover' defines it in terms of sales, so it has to be preferable to use the definitive word rather than one derived from it.

Lastly, the irrelevant parts of the report, from the point of view of the individual shareholder, can be separated from the relevant by the way in which the report is designed and laid out.

Information to employees

The reference to reports to employees raises a wider issue concerning their information needs as against those of the shareholders. One of the fundamental rules governing the provision of information on the company's affairs, is that information should be made equally available to all those with a legitimate interest in the business. In this way no privileged groups are created, who might be able to gain financially through knowing more about some aspects of the company's affairs than the shareholders in general.

Against this background, companies are now taking more trouble to brief their employees (some of whom may also be shareholders) on the financial state of the business and especially on the financial state of their particular part of the business. The information, which is relevant to the employees on a given site, is not likely to be relevant to the shareholders in general. It may, nevertheless, be price-sensitive if, for example, it involves revealing plans for investment or divestment. The employees start from the position of being more knowledgeable about their side of the business than the shareholders and they are better placed to ask well-directed questions of the management in order to add to that knowledge.

Insider trading

Access to information about a company which is not generally known does not of itself create a problem. It is only when that information is used to deal in the company's shares that the issue of insider trading arises. To prevent insider trading, the London Stock Exchange sets out model rules for companies to adopt in respect of dealings by directors, and many companies restrict the period during which directors can buy and sell their company's shares, even further than is provided for under those rules.

It is not only the directors, however, who know more than the shareholders in general about events within the company which may have a bearing on the value of its shares. To an extent, everyone who works in a company has access to more information than those outside it, and even a company's suppliers and customers could be in something of the same position. Thus the definition of who might be considered to be an insider is a difficult one. Equal access to all information about a company is an impossible aim, but the more widely such information can be made available, the less is the risk of inside knowledge being improperly used to gain a trading advantage.

Guidelines

Companies need to watch, therefore, that they do not inadvertently put some of their employees in a position to be accused of insider trading through their laudable efforts to keep them well briefed. This may become more of an issue in the European Union, if the Commission rules that the flow of information to employees should be augmented. In balancing the rights of employees to be kept informed on matters which directly affect them, against the rights of shareholders to parity of information, the guideline seems to me to be one of common sense.

It is in the interests of the company, and therefore of the

shareholders, that employees should be aware of the true state of that part of the business in which they work. As a result, there may be differences between the information given generally to shareholders and to specific groups of employees. The requirements are that the information should be relevant to the needs of both categories and that information which could reasonably be expected to affect the share price should be made generally available.

The Annual General Meeting

Chairmen report to their shareholders in writing twice a year, but at the Annual General Meeting they meet those who choose to attend face to face. The AGM is a formal occasion and it has essential business to conduct, such as the election of directors, the appointment of the auditors and the decision on the dividend. It also presents shareholders with an opportunity to enquire into the running of the business and the chairman with an opportunity to bring shareholders up to date with the company's progress. Chairmen who pride themselves on the speed with which their AGMs are concluded are ignoring the advantages to be won from encouraging shareholders to ask questions. Such questions give chairmen a feel for the issues which are on the minds of shareholders and in answering them they have the chance to put forward the company's point of view, persuasively and in a public forum.

Shareholders' questions

How shareholders' questions are answered at an AGM is a matter of individual choice for chairmen. I preferred to take them all myself and if I did not know the answer, I asked the questioner to talk to the appropriate board member after the meeting. It is less easy to keep the meeting under control if the board is turned into a panel and especially if the auditors are to be brought into the act as well, as some have suggested. The other advantage for chairmen of answering shareholders' questions personally is that it ensures that they prepare thoroughly for the meeting. This preparatory work gives them a useful point of contact with a number of executives, and the most certain way of ensuring that you understand issues fully is to stand ready to answer questions on them.

It is encouraging that one of the proposals put forward in the first edition of this book, for making better use of the opportunity to ask questions at AGMs, has been acted upon. The suggestion was that shareholders should be able to send in written questions, in addition to being able to ask them at the meeting itself, and that all shareholders should receive a summary of questions asked and answers given after the meeting. Grand Metropolitan, following their policy of looking for ways of strengthening their links with their shareholders, encouraged written questions at their 1993 AGM and received 320 individual replies. The company then sent all its shareholders a booklet summarising the major questions raised and the answers given to them by the chairman. This initiative showed that shareholders are interested in debating such matters as strategy, governance and the future direction of their companies if given the opportunity.

Private shareholders should recognise that, although they may not have voting power, they have considerable moral power and that chairmen and their boards will do their best to respond positively to well-directed proposals or criticisms from them.

The powers of the chairman

The course of a general meeting is not necessarily predictable; consequently, chairmen need to know just what their powers are and to have agreed with the company secretary how a demand for a poll or a serious interruption will be dealt with. It is also advisable to have outside legal advice on tap as well. This is because the powers of a chairman in general meeting are not all that clearly defined, as is apparent from the case of *Byng* v. *London Life Association* (1988). There, the court found first in favour of the chairman of London Life – a decision which was then reversed in the Court of Appeal.

Byng v. London Life Association

The account of the case, which appeared in the Weekly Law Reports of 28 April 1989, merits reading, since it covers a number of aspects of the powers of a chairman under the common law. What happened, briefly, was that London Life had called a general meeting to pass a special resolution. The room in the Barbican, in which the meeting was to be held, proved to be too small for the numbers attending and the audio-visual links with the overflow rooms failed to work properly. The chairman, therefore, decided to adjourn the meeting until later in the day and to reconvene in a larger room at the Café Royal. He made this decision without taking a vote.

His action in adjourning was challenged on the grounds that he should have taken a vote on the adjournment, that by changing the meeting-place and time he was preventing a number of members from taking part in the debate and voting, and that he should have abandoned the meeting, reconvening it at a later date.

On the first point, the company's articles laid down that a meeting could be adjourned by a vote. The question was, therefore, whether the chairman's common law power to adjourn could override the company's articles. The Court of Appeal held:

> That, although a motion to adjourn could not be put to the meeting as many entitled to vote would have been excluded, the common law permitted the chairman to adjourn the meeting and article 18 did not preclude the chairman from exercising the common law power to adjourn the meeting in circumstances where the views of the members could not be ascertained.

On the central point, however, of whether the meeting should have been abandoned and a new one convened at a later date, the Court of Appeal found against the chairman of London Life. This was on the basis that the matter to be voted on was not so urgent that it justified effectively excluding a number of members from attending and voting. The Court of Appeal held that, 'Although the chairman acted in good faith, he was under a duty to act reasonably with a view to facilitate the limited purpose for which the power to adjourn the meeting existed.'

Thus the chairman has powers, but they are restricted and can only be used to further the purpose for which they exist. In this case, the purpose was to enable more members to take part in the debate than had proved possible in the Barbican; in the court's view, that purpose was not adequately achieved by the chairman's decision. What is not referred to in any of the reports on the case is the relentless pressure which chairmen are under in these circumstances. They have to make the best decisions they can in the brief time they have for consultation and reflection, possibly in situations of considerable confusion.

Points of guidance

Nevertheless, there are useful points of guidance which arise from *Byng* v. *London Life Association*. In the first place, the case confirmed that chairmen have powers, under the common law, to take such steps as may be necessary to enable meetings to achieve their purpose. They can and should, for example, adjourn a meeting to prevent violence, although the definition of violence seems also to be a matter of judgement. A judge commented in an earlier case, Megarry J. in *John* v. *Rees* (1970) Ch 345, 'Obviously there is no duty to adjourn if the violence consists of no more than a few technical assaults.' The same judge referred to the need for a chairman at an unruly meeting to have 'the voice of a good schoolmaster'.

Second, the case has established that the members at a general meeting do not all have to be in the same room, provided that they are able to participate in the proceedings as if they were. This raises some interesting possibilities for the future, such as using tele-conferencing to allow members to take part in general meetings at a distance.

Other practical points on holding AGMs include the advisability of having both room to spare and an efficient system of registration, the need to have the company secretary, legal adviser and the articles of association all within easy reach – and the advantage of possessing a stentorian voice.

Correspondence with shareholders

While the AGM provides shareholders with the opportunity to put questions to their chairmen once a year, they can do so at any time by writing to them. Judging by the way in which some shareholders address their letters – 'for the chairman's personal attention only' and so on – they expect them to be diverted down the line and doubt if they will reach their destination. In this, they underrate the importance which chairmen attach to the views of individual shareholders.

Some of the points raised by shareholders with chairmen may best be answered by the appropriate executive; even so, chairmen will be aware of what caused the letter to be written in the first place and of the nature of the reply. Cranks apart, most shareholders only take up their pens when they feel strongly enough about something to overcome the inertia of writing. Chairmen need to accord the same sense of priority to seeing that their letters are answered.

THE CHAIRMAN AND THE FINANCIAL INSTITUTIONS

In representing the company to the financial institutions, the chairman has to ensure that good working links are maintained with three constituencies: financial analysts, institutional shareholders and sources of finance. The importance of these links has grown in line with the greater interest now shown in the activities of companies and the increased incidence of bids and buy-outs. The responsibility for keeping these links in good working order is the chairman's, even though personal involvement in so doing will be limited, particularly in a company whose shares are widely traded. The need to keep in close touch with the financial institutions and with those who comment on the business scene has meant that more companies now have staff specifically assigned to this activity and that they make greater use of outside specialists in the field of investor relations.

Basic principles

The more the responsibility for contacts with the financial institutions is diffused within a company, the more important it becomes for chairmen to ensure that the principles which determine the nature of those contacts are upheld. I would put forward two basic principles governing the provision of information on the company and I have already referred to them. First, that the company should be as open as it sensibly can be about the financial state of the business and, second, that it should treat equally all those whom it has a duty to keep informed.

These two principles can only be put into practice if there is an efficient communication chain from the company to shareholders, commentators and markets. Their application requires that the information provided by the company should be accurately inter-preted and broadly disseminated. It is here that the financial analysts have come to play such a key role.

Financial analysts

The deregulation of markets has moved analysts, or the best of them, to the centre of the stage. Competition between those firms which offer a service in the buying and selling of shares has become severe. They compete on the basis of the judgement of their principals and the quality of the research which lies behind their judgement.

It is the analysts who carry out research and who provide professional assessments of companies in a way which was rare in less competitive days. Financial analysts who become expert in particular companies or company sectors carry considerable influence, not only directly through their recommendations to buy, hold or sell shares, but also as a source of information for the media.

As chairman, I met with financial analysts as a group on the announcement of the company's annual and half-yearly results. Originally, we met with the press first on these occasions and the analysts afterwards, leaving the more demanding meeting to the last.

More recently, we changed the order round, recognising that the press wanted to be able to consult selected analysts before going into print. All of which underlines the importance of a company's relationship with the analysts who follow its fortunes. This relationship raises a difficult and sensitive issue for chairmen.

Analysts' forecasts

Both the company and the analyst have a common interest in the relative accuracy of the latter's forecasts. It does the company and its shareholders no good if the expectations of analysts are unreasonably high, so that a respectable result from the company's viewpoint is greeted by the stock market as disappointing. On the other hand, if their expectations are too low, the company's shares will be undervalued, which will advantage buyers at the expense of sellers.

Equally, analysts cannot afford to be too far out in their predictions, given that it is on this that their careers depend. The danger of this symbiotic relationship is that the dividing line between answering the analyst's legitimate questions and steering the analyst towards a particular conclusion will be crossed. The contacts which companies have with analysts are ultimately in the name of their chairmen, and so chairmen need to be able to reassure themselves that the line is being held and that an improper degree of guidance is not being given.

Analysts gain their competitive advantage by being better informed about a company than their rivals. Analysts, therefore, have an interest in acquiring information which is not generally available and will understandably seek to gain it. What matters to the company is that they should do so through their analytical skill, in deducing more than their competitors about the company's prospects from the way in which they piece together the same facts and figures, rather than from privileged information.

The other way in which they can gain a competitive edge is through their ability to assess the competence of the people running a company. What counts is the professionalism and the judgement of the analysts with whom the company deals; it is up to the chairman to know what their individual standing is within their circle.

Analysts' skills

Analysts are important to companies and to their chairmen, because of their role in interpreting information about the company and in passing it on to other audiences. Professional analysts understand the structure of the businesses which they follow and so can assess what effect a particular event – a change in taxation, the loss of a market, the launch of a new product and so on – is likely to have on a company's earnings in the short and long term. It was this more accurate assessment of cause and effect which was lacking before the rise of the professional analyst.

In addition, as communicators, analysts are the main link between the company as the source of information and those who have an interest in acting on that information, whether they are financial institutions, stockbrokers' clients or the media. Their role is, therefore, central and deserves to be treated as such by chairmen.

Institutional shareholders

The company's links with its institutional shareholders are sufficiently different from those with individual shareholders for them to be discussed under a separate heading. Institutional shareholders have a decisive voice in a company's affairs through their voting power. The relationship between chairmen and their companies' largest share-holders is one which needs to be fostered on a continuing basis. Relationships cannot be established instantly, when the need arises from a company's point of view. The contacts between companies and their larger institutional investors will as far as possible be direct and personal, involving chairmen and their senior colleagues. In addition, however, select gatherings may be arranged from time to time for a few institutional guests to meet the chairman, chief executive or finance director of a particular company – usually over lunch.

Free lunches

The problem about such gatherings is that they come – in the words of an investment fund manager, quoted by *The Financial Times* (1 June 1987) – 'perilously close to passing price-sensitive information to a privileged group of investors who are given insights not available to the wider body of shareholders'. The same fund manager went on to say that, to many investors, this would be the only point in attending meetings of this kind. A dilemma for chairmen, who equally are guests on these occasions, is that they wish to strengthen their links with the institutions, whether they are actual or potential investors, but they do not wish to put them at the same time in a privileged position.

One solution, which has been canvassed, is that companies should limit their contacts with all investor audiences to the period immediately after the announcement of the annual and half-year results, in the light of the now tighter rules on insider trading. This is, perhaps, unnecessarily restrictive and would in any case run counter to the general aim of maintaining a flow of information. The dilemma for companies is particularly acute during the period between the publication of their interim and their final results.

In the five months or so between putting out their final and their interim results, chairmen have the opportunity through their annual reports and their AGMs to bring shareholders and analysts up to date with the activities and prospects of their companies. They have no similar opportunities during the longer gap between the interim and final results. One answer would be for British companies to move to quarterly reporting in line with their American counterparts. There is no sign as yet, however, that British shareholders regard the additional costs of quarterly reporting, which they would ultimately bear, as being worth the return. A half-way house would be for companies to publish an extra trading statement between their interim and final results, as some professional financial communication firms have urged.

A more effective way of filling any communication gaps which may exist at present, might be to hold fewer select gatherings and offer more opportunities for wider audiences of investors and analysts to hear presentations by companies and to have the chance of questioning those who are responsible for running them.

Formal company presentations

The investing institutions are on record as saying that what they would appreciate would be more company presentations, which are open to those interested and which are formally structured. Such presentations would be designed to give factual information about the company and its objectives and to provide an opportunity to meet and question the management team. It would be in the interests of companies to move in this direction and away from attendance at exclusive luncheon parties, with all the misgivings to which they can give rise.

It is clearly important for companies, the majority of whose shares are held by institutions, to keep in close and regular touch with those shareholders who, between them, control the company. It is also important for wider reasons, because it is the institutions who are in a position to bring about change in the boardrooms of companies which are failing to achieve adequate results.

Sources of finance

The relationship between companies and those who provide them with financial services of all kinds has altered dramatically in the last few years. This is as a result of deregulation, the merging of financial service companies into larger groupings and the internationalisation of financial markets. The consequence is that the market for the provision of financial services has become more competitive and more specialised. At the same time, many of the larger companies have developed their own treasury departments in-house, which are often separate profit centres as well.

There are, therefore, two pressures on company treasurers to treat each financial transaction on its own merits and to conclude it with whichever finance house can offer the best terms on the day. One is that each finance house will tend to have its own special area of expertise, which means going to different firms for different types of business. The other is that the treasurers want to get the finest of possible rates from the point of view of attaining their own budget targets. Whereas, in the past, a company had a relationship with its main bankers which was built up over time, companies now may be dealing with a range of financial firms and have no long-standing links with any of them.

Chairmen are rightly concerned lest, in a predatory world, the bankers to whom they look for financial backing may be equally prepared to finance an unwanted bid for them. They are entitled to look for loyalty from their bankers, but their bankers are similarly entitled to look to them for loyalty in return.

This presents chairmen with two options. They can establish long-term relationships with particular financial firms and those who manage them. Thereby they will know that they can rely on the support of their bankers should they be in need of funds or under external attack. Alternatively, they can encourage their finance departments to shop around in order to get the keenest possible price for each transaction. Chairmen and their boards have to decide which of these two approaches best meets the needs of their companies.

THE CHAIRMAN AND THE MEDIA

It is part of the chairman's job 'to represent the company properly to the outside world'. This includes being prepared to appear on television and to give interviews on the radio or to the press, as the occasion demands. The main point is that in doing so chairmen are representing their companies and not – deliberately anyway – promoting themselves. The decision, therefore, whether or not to take part in a programme has to be based on the benefit which taking part will bring to the company, or the possible disbenefit of turning the offer down. It is unlikely that anything will be lost by not taking part in a particular programme; it is better to decline to do so than to risk becoming involved in a feature which may have been designed to show the company in a poor light.

The representational role is one in which chairmen will find professional help and advice invaluable. The back-up for chairmen in their public relations work may come from outside the company, from within it, or from a combination of the two. What chairmen need are competent practitioners in whom they have confidence and to whom they can turn for instant guidance. One of the characteristics of the representational role is that chairmen can be called upon to fulfil it at short notice. Chairmen have to decide which aspects of the role they are good at, what training and experience they need and when they should leave the task to someone else.

Television

Television is the most exacting medium and the one where experience is the greatest help. When chairmen appear on television they give a wide audience an impression of themselves as people and, therefore, an impression of the company they represent. There could even be rare occasions when the way they come across on television might prove to be crucial in commercial terms. If some disaster has struck the company, the chairman in commenting on it has to convey that the company has matters under control and is taking every possible action to mitigate its consequences. Provided the chairman creates that impression, the company will win public support and sympathy and will be left to get on with managing the emergency. If the chairman's response appears to be uncertain, then the opposite will happen, making the task of recovery all the harder.

Such extreme situations aside, television appearances are more likely to affect the public image of the company than the share price. It is necessary, therefore, for companies to have a view as to the picture of themselves which they aim to present and to co-ordinate all the different aspects of their external relations to that end. Television, more than any other medium, tends to focus on personalities rather than events and institutions. To that extent, it is difficult for chairmen to be certain that they are putting over the company rather than themselves. I used to encourage myself with the thought that my name was eponymous with one of our main brands and, in consequence, any appearance on television would, however modestly, reinforce the company's advertising.

It is also worth bearing in mind that employees and customers are more likely to see chairmen on television than to read about them in the press, or to hear them on radio. It matters to employees that the company for which they work should be presented positively on their television screens; thus effective appearances by the chairman and others representing the company are important to everyone associated with the enterprise.

Videos

A natural extension of appearing on television is for chairmen to make use of video programmes to reach specific audiences. The technical advances in the production of videos in the last few years have been impressive. It is a technique which is now widely employed for teaching and it opens up a range of new ways of putting over information about the company. Videos are mainly used for internal communications and offer particular advantages to international companies; but they can also be addressed to shareholders and customers or shown at investor presentations.

It is helpful in making videos if chairmen establish a relationship with a particular production team, so that they get to know each other's ways. The great plus of videos is that they enable chairmen or chief executives to be multiplied on the screen as many times as required and to appear at any number of sites simultaneously.

Another important advantage of the video, as a means of communication, is that it enables chairmen to put across their messages in the form which suits them. Chairmen have little say over the nature of the television programmes in which they may appear; this is why it is as well to clear the ground rules with the producer before deciding whether to take part.

Radio

Radio programmes on company affairs usually provide their listeners with factual information, as they do when a company's results are announced, or they feature aspects of business life. Taking part in radio programmes is not, therefore, likely to have much commercial impact on the company. However, the way in which the chairman or chief executive comes across in them does give listeners an impression of what their company might be like. Some of the advantages of radio programmes are that their intent in discussing business affairs is normally serious rather than partisan and that they are in a better position to give time to an issue than is television. Lastly, radio interviewers and producers are, in my experience, thoroughly professional in the way in which they present their programmes.

The press

Variations in professional standards are widest among the press. The reputations of the journals themselves vary, as do those of their contributors. At the top of the scale, there are experienced business journalists, writing in newspapers and magazines, whose articles on companies and on their management are well informed and authoritative. At the other end, there are reporters with no business grounding, whose comments are either unpredictable or biased. Chairmen need to acquire a feel for the place on the scale of those journalists who approach them for interviews or who ring them up – usually when they are at home.

Press reporting does have an influence on the standing of a company, on the price of a company's shares and on business issues. Although regular investors may rely on the research and recommendations of analysts, enough investors follow the financial advice columns in the press for them to be able to move share prices. Once that movement is established, it tends to go unjustifiably far before reality reasserts itself. In the same way, once a journal has formed a view for good or ill about the management of a company, it will be slow to change it.

I mention business issues because in a contested takeover bid, for example, the line taken by the press can influence the government over decisions which it may have to make in relation to the bid. Their line can influence the public mood towards the bid as well. In these ways the attitude of the press may affect both the chances of a bid succeeding and the cost of it doing so. Equally, on broader issues such as those related to public health and the environment, the press is in a position to mount campaigns which can directly affect companies and their markets.

A further reason why the press has a lasting influence on businesses is that newspaper and magazine articles are kept on file and are referred back to, both by the media themselves and by financial commentators and analysts. This is why inaccurate or slanted articles are damaging; even if corrections are subsequently printed, they are rarely filed with the errors which gave rise to them.

The relationship between chairmen and the press is, therefore, important and it helps if chairmen get to know personally some of the leading figures among business journalists. It also assists in building the right relationship with the press if chairmen are known to be reasonably accessible and straightforward in their response to questions.

CONCLUSIONS ON THE REPRESENTATIONAL ROLE

The importance of the role

It is essential that companies should present their past record and their future opportunities positively to the outside world. Markets, and those whose comments move markets, evaluate a company on the basis of what they believe it has achieved and will achieve. This evaluation is based on their necessarily limited knowledge of the business and of how it is run. It is the company's job to correct any misapprehensions in their assessments and to provide a rounded picture of the company and its prospects. The outside world judges companies by the kinds of business they are in, but above all by the competence and flair of the people who are running them. The chairman has the responsibility of conveying to the public the ambitions of the company and the abilities of its management.

The standing of a company and the way it is regarded externally are crucial for a number of reasons. In the first place, it is vital to shareholders that the market should appreciate, as nearly as possible, the true worth of their investment in the business. It is the job of the chairman and the board to see that the price at which the company's shares are traded is based on an adequate understanding of the company's potential.

The dual market

One of the problems over the stock market valuation of companies is that there can now be two distinct markets in a company's shares. There is the market in which its shares are traded alongside those of other companies and valued in the same way as their shares. Then there is the separate market for the control of assets, which is triggered by bids and rumours of bids and which will value the business on a different set of criteria. The consequences of having a dual market of this kind have been thoroughly analysed in an important paper by Jonathan Charkham on the market for the control of companies. As he says, 'There is always a bid premium over a pure trading price simply because control of a company is worth more than the sum total of the value of the shares without control.'

The relevance of the dual market to the price of a company's shares is that there will inevitably be a sizeable gap between their respective methods of valuing companies. All that shareholders can reasonably expect of chairmen and boards is that the shares of their companies should be realistically valued, whichever of the two markets they happen to be in.

The standing of the company

The standing of a company in the market-place and the tone of the public comment about it are important not only in relation to the share price. They have a bearing on the company's ability to recruit and on the quality of those who apply for jobs. They also matter to the employees, since the people who work in a company need to feel that their contribution to its progress is being properly recognised. It is natural for everyone to want to be part of a successful enterprise, and success in that sense is measured by the outside world.

Although it is usually chairmen who take the lead in representing the company externally, it is a task in which they need to be backed by everyone in the business who is in a position to help. It is also an advantage if chairmen can select professionals in the field of public relations, who think along the same lines as they do, and with whom they find it easy to work.

Chairmen then have to decide on the best means of communicating with a particular audience. The main distinction is between communications which originate from within the company, for which it is solely responsible, and those which originate from outside the business, to which the chairman responds. While the messages about a company conveyed, say, in a chairman's answers to questions from an interviewer, are less under their control than a prepared pronouncement, they may, for that very reason, carry more weight with the audience.

Consistency and continuity

The central point is that it is for chairmen and their supporting staff to orchestrate the way in which the company presents itself, so that it takes advantage of all the opportunities which are open to it and, more importantly, that the responses to those opportunities are co-ordinated. The picture which the company presents through all its external communications, intended as such or otherwise, has, above all, to be consistent, if it is to be persuasive.

Chairmen should acquire as much practical experience as possible in carrying out their representational role. This is in order not only to build on that experience, but also to find out where their particular strengths lie. At the same time, taking part in programmes of various kinds enables chairmen to learn something about those who present them. When chairmen are seeking public support for their companies, it will help if they are respected by the media and can discuss the issues at stake with people whom they already know. A further point is that external contacts of all kinds, whether with the media or with shareholders, cannot be switched on or off to suit the company. The external relations programme has to be a continuing one, if it is to be effective.

Responsiveness

The emphasis in this chapter has been on what chairmen say or write in their representational role. But the role also consists of listening to what it is that the outside world wants to know about the company and its activities. Communications should flow in both directions. Some companies go to considerable lengths to encourage questions by employees and shareholders and to have them answered authoritatively.

That approach makes it clear that the company is willing to explain its policies and actions; it also means that the concerns of individual questioners are answered directly and precisely. The problem with general company pronouncements is that too much of their content may be irrelevant to individual members of the audience. The opportunity, particularly for employees, to question those with the power of decision in a company is important. Although the video is a powerful means of presenting the company's point of view, its limitation is that it is a one-way transmission and it does not provide for questions and debate.

The rules

The primary rules for chairmen in representing their companies to the outside world are openness and even-handedness. The company should make available as much information as it reasonably can; this information should be provided equally to all those who have a claim to be kept informed. Since a number of people will be involved in representing the company under the chairman's leadership, chairmen have to make certain that they are all playing to their rules and presenting the same picture of the business.

How much chairmen do publicly in representing their companies has to be their own decision and they have to do it in their own way. Coaching and advice are helpful, type-casting is not; chairmen need to develop their own natural style. What the chairman's audiences are looking for is evidence that the company is competently run and that the chairman is both confident and in control.

CHAPTER 9

THE SOCIAL RESPONSIBILITIES OF COMPANIES

Few trends could so thoroughly undermine the very foundations of
our free society as the acceptance by corporate officials of a social
responsibility other than to make as much money for their
stockholders as possible.
Milton Friedman, *Capitalism and Freedom*

DEFINITIONS OF SOCIAL RESPONSIBILITY

Chairmen and companies do not lack for advice on their responsibilities to society. Professor Milton Friedman measures social
responsibility in earnings per share. The US Chamber of Commerce,
on the other hand, suggested in 1973 that companies should consider
restructuring their objectives, 'so that social goals are put on a par
with economic goals'. What these two divergent approaches to the
question of social responsibility demonstrate is that the responsibilities of companies to society are difficult to define. In addition, they
do not stand still; they are continually evolving.

It is precisely because social responsibility is a woolly term, that it
is important for boards to decide what social policy their companies
should follow – and companies have social policies, whether or not
they are thought through deliberately. In the absence of a positive lead
from the chairman and the board, the company's attitude towards its
social responsibilities will appear confused to those inside and outside
the company.

To be fair to Professor Friedman, his definition of social
responsibility arises out of a discussion of the importance of
maintaining political freedom. In pursuit of that aim, he would restrict
companies to a narrowly defined commercial role, leaving the
interaction between business and society to the political process. The
difficulty about the Friedman approach in practice is its deceptive
simplicity. It is not possible to isolate the economic elements of
business decisions from their social consequences, because companies

are part of the social system. Even the concept of making as much money for shareholders as possible begs the question – over what period of time?

The aim of maximising profits next year, or the year after, is an objective which can be translated directly into management action. Once the time horizon is extended to five or ten years, as it has to be with a continuing business, then maximising profits as a goal becomes of limited operational use. If the income of future shareholders is to be assured, resources will have to be invested, not just in machinery and buildings but in people and their training, and in maintaining or enhancing the company's reputation. Investing in people and in the standing of the company involves social as well as commercial judgements. The board has to hold the balance between profit now and profit in the future. The further a company looks ahead, the more difficult it becomes, in holding that balance, to maintain a simple separation between economic and social goals.

Shareholders' objectives differ

A further complication is that Professor Friedman assumes that shareholders share a common objective: that the company should make as much money as possible. In practice, as chairmen are well aware, shareholders have differing views on how companies should make· money and on how they should distribute it. Their objectives differ and they are not confined to furthering the strictly economic role of companies. I was regularly asked at annual general meetings about the company's policy on the support it gave to good causes.

Shareholder interest in the sense of social responsibility shown by companies is growing and some institutional investors, such as foundations and academic bodies, may well put the social goals of a company on a par with its economic goals. The launch of ethical and environmental unit trusts is evidence of the growing concern of shareholders for the behaviour of the companies in which they invest.

Recognising the social dimension

It would simplify the position for companies if they could choose one of two ways of recognising the social dimension in business decisions. The first would be for them to concentrate on running their businesses efficiently. Then they would either allocate a proportion of their profits to some agency which would make the social judgements for them or distribute as much as possible to the shareholders, who would make the social judgements for themselves.

The alternative would be for the board to regard social aims as inseparable from business aims, as enlightened industrialists did in the nineteenth century. Most companies plan to steer a middle course between these two extremes, not keeping the social dimension completely at arm's length, but having a social policy which is distinct from their commercial policy. The aim of this chapter is to provide chairmen with some pointers to help them and their boards decide what course their company should follow in framing a social policy.

WHY IS SOCIAL RESPONSIBILITY ON THE AGENDA?

Business success

There are a number of reasons why social responsibility has become such a live issue for boards. One is that business in the developed world has proved remarkably successful at meeting society's material needs. When economic growth and a higher standard of living were overriding aims, the contribution of companies to the attainment of those aims was well understood. Now, economic growth as an unqualified aim is increasingly being questioned, although the questioners often take the material benefits of growth for granted. At the same time, much more is now being learnt about the side-effects of economic growth and development on the environment. Just as companies have to balance the demands of the future against those of the present, so does society, and communities are becoming more conscious of their responsibilities to future generations.

Company power

Another reason is the apparent increase in the power of companies, particularly of large international companies, over recent years. They are seen as being capable of changing the societies in which they carry on their business, for better or worse. Indeed, there is now a greater degree of interdependence between business and governments, since governmental goals can often only be achieved through the co-operation of companies. Governments, for example, can only attain their aims in such fields as training and equal opportunities by working with and through companies.

Expectations

There has also been a general rise in the expectations of society, which has its roots in better communications, in a greater awareness of what is taking place in the wider world and in a more questioning approach to accepted ideas. All of which challenge the traditional view of companies simply as providers of goods and services.

COMPANY LAW AND SOCIAL RESPONSIBILITY

One of the problems during a period of rapid economic and social change is that the legal framework, within which companies operate, tends to become out of date and out of line with the ways in which boards act, let alone the ways in which society expects them to act.

The Watkinson Report

The Watkinson Report on *The responsibilities of the British public company*, to which I have already referred, gave a strong lead as to the direction company law should take to narrow the gap between the legal obligations of companies and the duties of boards, as board members see them:

> We think that the Government might consider, as part of their doctrine of wider disclosure, a general legislative encouragement for companies, to recognise duties and obligations (within the context of the objects for which the company was established) arising from the company's relationship with creditors, suppliers, customers, employees and society at large; and in so doing to exercise their best judgment to strike a balance between the interests of the aforementioned groups and between the interests of the proprietors of the company.

Striking the balance

The Report's concept of striking a balance goes to the heart of the exercise of social responsibility. It is the board's job to reach decisions and in so doing to take account of the interests which will be affected by those decisions and to give due weight to them. The law sets the framework within which the balance of interests has to be struck. Britain, for example, was behind the rest of Western Europe in accepting that companies had obligations to employees as well as to shareholders. Since the Watkinson Report was published, directors of

British companies have been required, as part of the duty which they owe to the company, to have regard to the interests of employees in general (s.309, Company Act 1985).

The moral imperative

It is important that company law should be updated to reflect the changing pattern of responsibilities accepted by boards, in order to protect those companies who have moved in advance of the law and to raise the general standard of company behaviour. Nevertheless, the law cannot be expected to give a lead over the responsibilities of boards. The law consolidates changes in business conduct that have already occurred and represents enforceable standards rather than best practice. As the Watkinson Report says, 'One cannot look to the Companies Acts to provide "a moral imperative". This must be one of the duties of companies and their boards.'

In carrying out that duty, chairmen and their boards will have to decide on their definition of social responsibility.

WHAT IS SOCIAL RESPONSIBILITY?

A contract with society

The broadest way of defining social responsibility is to say that the continued existence of companies is based on an implied agreement between business and society. In effect, companies are licensed by society to provide the goods and services which society needs. The freedom of operation of companies is, therefore, dependent on their delivering whatever balance of economic and social benefits society currently expects of them. The problem for companies is that the balance of needs and benefits is continually changing and there is no accepted way of measuring those changes.

To start with, companies are expected to meet society's demands for goods and services, to provide employment, to contribute to the exchequer and to operate efficiently at a profit. There is no conflict between social responsibility and the obligation on companies to use scarce resources efficiently and to be profitable – an unprofitable business is a drain on society. The essence of the contract between society and business is that companies shall not pursue their immediate profit objectives at the expense of the longer-term interests of the community.

Basic company responsibilities

In practice, it is possible to distinguish three levels of company responsibility. The primary level comprises the company's responsibilities to meet its material obligations to shareholders, employees, customers, suppliers and creditors, to pay its taxes and to meet its statutory duties. The sanctions against failure to match up to these relatively easily defined and measured responsibilities are provided by competition and by the law.

Responsibility for actions

The next level of responsibility is concerned with the direct results of the actions of companies in carrying out their primary task and includes making the most of the community's human resources and avoiding damage to the environment. At this level, it is not enough to say that pollution or noise levels meet legal requirements. What is here required of companies is that they should be attempting to minimise any adverse effects of their actions, rather than adhering to the lowest acceptable standard.

At least at these two levels of responsibility, companies can define the issues in question and their boards can decide where to strike the balance between the different interests involved. It will also be possible to make estimates, however rough, of the costs which will be incurred and of the benefits which will accrue, since both costs and benefits will be largely internal to the firm.

Responsibility for consequences of actions

Beyond these two levels, there is a much less well-defined area of responsibility, which takes in the interaction between business and society in a wider sense. How far has business a responsibility to maintain the framework of the society in which it operates and how far should business reflect society's priorities rather than its own commercial priorities?

At this level, companies have to look outwards at the changing terms on which society will license them to carry on their activities, rather than inwards at their own performance, as is implied by the other two levels of responsibility. The definition of responsibility moves further out of the hands of companies at this stage, because business decisions are like stones thrown into a pool, which is society, and companies are asked to take account of the ripples they cause as they move outwards to the shore. This requires companies to envisage the wider consequences of their decisions and to build that awareness into their decision-making processes.

DIFFICULTIES OF DEFINITION

Who is 'society'?

I have used the word 'society' as if it were clear what it means, but this turns on how widely society is to be defined. If, for example, a factory is dirtying the neighbourhood washing by the discharge from its chimney, the local community is likely to press for the company to recognise its responsibilities to society, that is to say, to them, by ceasing to pollute the neighbourhood.

One way of achieving this may be to erect a taller chimney on the boiler house, planners permitting, so as to throw the smuts into the upper atmosphere. This may meet the needs of 'society' locally, but 'society' as consumers of the products made by the factory will find themselves contributing to the cost of the chimney, and 'society' in some country outside Britain can now expect to receive the factory's imperfectly combusted discharge.

From the point of view of those living near to the factory the problem would be solved, because their washing would now be cleaner. But the board of the company concerned cannot take quite such a parochial view of its responsibilities. It will have to weigh up the consequences of its actions on the different sectors of society which will be affected by them before it can decide on the best way of solving its pollution problem.

The concern expressed today about the worldwide consequences of damaging the environment is an example of the changing terms of the licence from society under which companies operate. In the past, that concern would have centred on the local effects of pollution; now companies are expected to answer for the international effects of any pollution they may cause. The key point is that boards, in framing their social policies, need to be clear who, in any particular instance, they mean by society.

Who are the employees?

The same kind of definitional problem arises when a company considers what its obligations are to its employees. To the representatives of the employees at the bargaining table, the definition of who is an employee is straightforward: employees are the people who chose them to represent their interests. To the board, the definition is less straightforward. The board may have to make investment decisions which will reduce employment in the short term, but will result in better value to customers, so making the jobs of the smaller work-force more secure.

In making such decisions, the board will be balancing its responsibilities to present employees against those to future employees, employees on pension, employees as consumers and employees who are either directly or indirectly shareholders. At the bargaining table only the interests of present employees will be represented, but the board has to have some regard for the interests of these other categories of employee as well.

No universal guidelines

Because the factors which boards have to weigh in coming to their decisions are so complex, there can be no universal guidelines on how a company should take account of its social responsibilities. All that generalised definitions of social responsibility can achieve is to indicate the kind of considerations boards should have in mind in arriving at a social policy.

Chairmen and boards have to come to their individual conclusions on what constitutes social responsibility in the particular circumstances of their own companies. The priority for some will be to remain in business. Failing companies will rightly have a different set of social priorities from successful ones. Boards need to define how they currently see the social responsibilities of their companies, so that there should be no confusion down the line over aims and so that they can keep a check on their progress towards those aims.

WHO IS RESPONSIBLE FOR SOCIAL POLICY?

The responsibility for defining the company's social policy and for supervising its implementation rests with the chairman and the board. It is easy, for example, for a board to agree on a policy of non-discrimination in recruitment, but their responsibilities do not end with passing an irreproachable board resolution to that effect. The place where discrimination is most likely to occur is not in the personnel department but at the factory gate, where would-be applicants first present themselves. It is the board's responsibility to initiate the company's policy on non-discrimination and it is equally the board's responsibility to see that it is followed through.

It is by its decisions and actions that a company's policy on social responsibility is ultimately defined. It is helpful to everyone concerned if the board agrees a written social policy, to which ready reference can be made. The test, however, which managers will apply to board statements on social responsibility is how far adherence to them is recognised in decisions on their pay and promotion.

The board has the task of balancing the different interests which companies have to take into account in arriving at such policy decisions as whether to enter a new line of business or to close an existing one. Managers in their turn have to balance the social objectives of their companies with meeting their budgets. The dilemma is the same at the policy level and at the level of implementation; that is, what weight should be given to which business and social pressures?

PRESSURE GROUPS

Here it is necessary to touch on the rise of organised interest groups, because of the part they can play in attempting to influence company decisions with consequences in the social or environmental field. The essential point about pressure groups is that they are single-minded. They are formed to pursue a particular purpose, often a negative one – to campaign against the closure of a factory, for example. They carry no responsibility for finding a better solution to the problems which gave rise to the proposed closure; they are simply against it.

The ethical superiority of the uninvolved

This narrow focus gives interest groups a debating advantage over company boards, who cannot evade the responsibility for taking decisions in the same way. In an authoritative book on business ethics called *Hard Problems of Management*, Mark Pastin has perceptively referred to 'the ethical superiority of the uninvolved', and chairmen will recognise that there is a good deal of it about. Pressure groups are skilled at seizing the moral high ground and arguing that the judgement of boards is at best biased and at worst influenced solely by private gain, because boards have a direct commercial interest in their decisions. But boards are also responsible for arriving at business decisions and for taking account of the various interests which will be affected by them; the uninvolved are not.

Public relations

Boards should consider doing more to explain the complexities which lie behind major business decisions. Interest groups aim to simplify and to distil all the arguments down to a question of right or wrong. If decisions were as straightforward as that, boards would not need to spend much time on them. The problem for an interest group is that once the wider implications of business decisions are brought into the discussion, the narrow preoccupation which gives the group its cohesion is weakened.

The uninvolved will also argue that information and comment from companies is just an exercise in public relations, using those words in a pejorative sense. Public relations, however, are an essential aspect of a company's links with society; what matters is the inspiration behind them which determines their trustworthiness.

Soundly based public relations involve listening first and then responding to whatever points have been raised. Interest groups have their part to play in that process, by making companies aware of the concerns which brought their group into existence. Companies should listen to them and be prepared to debate their arguments openly.

Boards, however, have to assess the costs and consequences of their decisions for all concerned; they need to recognise that the views of interest groups are part of their input to those decisions, but only a part. Not all the interests involved will have organised groups to represent them. For a company to go along with the demands of the most vocal or best-organised pressure group on an issue could be the easy way out of resolving a difficult conflict of interest, rather than an expression of social responsibility.

BUSINESS AND GOVERNMENT

A different kind of pressure on companies is for them to become actively involved in social fields like education or urban renewal, which are basically the responsibility of local and national government. There has been a move in Britain to reduce the role of the state and to encourage individuals to take more responsibility for shaping their own futures. Companies are expected to play their part in enabling this shift of authority – from government at the centre to local groups in their own community – to take place. In addition, governments in many countries are unable to resolve on their own the overwhelming problems arising from the twin processes of economic growth and decay.

Demands for company involvement

As an example, a 1968 article by Hazel Henderson in the *Harvard Business Review* had this to say of the demands which were being made on American companies at the time:

> Companies from A.T. & T. to Xerox have been urged [to accept] – and in many cases have willingly accepted – the challenges to educate our children, police our streets, clean up our polluted air and water, teach our disadvantaged citizens how to earn a living, rebuild our slums and even tell us how to run our cities more efficiently.

Since then the desire to see business 'as an all-purpose institution to right all social wrongs', to use John Diebold's phrase, may have moderated. Either way, the passage brings out some key issues which chairmen and their boards might have in mind in deciding how to respond to requests to take on the kind of responsibilities referred to in the article. Companies above all need to be clear on what terms they are prepared to become involved in fields for which government is responsible.

Terms of involvement

First, the choice of social goals has to be a political decision, which should not be delegated to business. Second, companies should not undertake governmental obligations for which they do not have matching authority. Lastly, the state should not be attempting to transfer its responsibilities to companies. What it can sensibly do is to look to companies to help it in carrying out some of its responsibilities, where companies have the capacity to do so.

There are government-backed social initiatives, such as vocational training for young people and the encouragement of new enterprises, which can only succeed with the active support and involvement of companies. They are examples of the interdependence of government and business, which in turn is the reason why companies cannot be neatly detached from the communities of which they are a part, as Professor Friedman's approach to social responsibility would demand.

COMPANY SOCIAL POLICIES

Because each company will approach its social responsibilities in its own way, discussion of these responsibilities has been in general terms. Boards will come to their own decisions on what their companies' social policies should be and on the principles on which they should be based. Nevertheless, it may be helpful to be rather more precise about how boards might set about defining their policies in this imprecise field.

Internal responsibilities

I drew a distinction earlier between three different levels of responsibility against which society could measure the actions of companies. The first was their responsibility to meet their material obligations and the second went beyond adherence to acceptable standards, in order to meet those set by best practice. A company's policy towards its responsibilities at these two levels is largely an internal matter. It is directed at making the most of the company's resources along with providing for their renewal and at minimising any negative effects of the company's actions on the community. This reflects the board's responsibility for the continuing health of the business, rather than its external involvement in the community.

There clearly is a social element in a company's policies at these levels. Behaving responsibly towards customers and suppliers makes business sense to any company thinking beyond the short term, but it is also one of the ways in which a company fulfils its obligations to the community. Involving employees in the decisions which directly affect them is an issue on which the European Social Charter places considerable importance, as I would. Nevertheless, it is more of a business responsibility than a social one. A company needs to have established a sense of common purpose among all those who make up the enterprise, if it is to carry out its primary task efficiently.

A company's responsibilities for matters affecting health, safety and the environment are another example of what is primarily a business responsibility, but one which entails particular duties to the community as well. The reason that companies have a special responsibility in these fields is that they know more about their products and processes than anyone else. They should, therefore, be the first to be aware of any hazards which could be attached to them.

If companies do have any doubts about the effects of their products on people or on the environment, they have a duty to share their concerns with the appropriate authorities as soon as they become aware of them. In consumer goods companies, this may result in expensive recalls of goods which are already in the shops, when the chances of a serious problem arising from their sale are minimal. The evidence is that companies which accept the costs of working to high standards of care, benefit from the loyalty of their customers.

A company's policies in respect of the first two levels of responsibility will reflect the views of its board on how they believe the business should be run. The board will arrive at them after weighing the interests of all those who have a stake in the continued success of the enterprise. It is when we move to the third level of responsibility – how far a company has a responsibility to maintain the structure of the society in which it operates – that the decisions for the chairman and the board become more difficult.

External responsibilities

The argument for companies to take on the responsibilities which society expects of them is largely one of self-interest. If a company invests in training its own employees, the costs are known and the return is direct to the company. If, however, a company gives managerial time to an educational partnership with the local schools from which it recruits, the returns are indirect and do not accrue solely to the company. This means that the board's decision on the amount of effort to put behind community initiatives has to be more a matter of judgement than of calculation.

First, the board needs to decide what resources of time and money it is prepared to put into meeting its external social responsibilities – those which are not an integral part of the business. Once that overall budgetary decision has been made, the board has to make choices and set priorities with the aim of concentrating the company's efforts where they can achieve the best results.

Choices and priorities

Boards have to choose from a formidable list of worthwhile social causes, all of which are looking for the backing of companies. I have already mentioned links with schools. That is a straightforward way for companies to involve themselves in their local communities, and both companies and schools have a common interest in enabling school pupils to make the most of their abilities. But staying within the educational field, companies in Britain are also being asked to find appropriate work experience places for pupils and their teachers, to provide teaching materials and equipment, to fund City Technology Colleges, to back enterprise schemes in schools and to sponsor students. All of these initiatives depend for their success on the active support of companies.

Education is not, however, the only claimant; there are a number of other causes, such as the regeneration of inner-city areas, the encouragement of new enterprises and the raising of standards of training, which are seeking company involvement under the banner of social responsibility.

Reference to the range of demands which are being made on companies in the social field could give the impression that the issue of how best to respond to them mainly faces larger companies. In fact, companies of any size can make a useful contribution to the community; thus businesses big and small need to decide what their policies are in this regard.

Some of the most effective education/business partnerships have been between one- and two-man businesses and their local schools. A small business can often give children a better insight into the world of work than a large company, because its activities are on a more human scale. The cost of this kind of social initiative to the one-man business is the time of its owner/manager, which is its main resource. The balance between the interests of the business and the interests of society has, therefore, to be as carefully struck by an owner/manager as by the board of a large corporation.

Need for structure

Large companies in their turn, particularly those with locations right across the country, are already involved to a greater or lesser extent in most of the social initiatives which have been mentioned. They have a particular need to establish clear social priorities, because the execution of those policies will be local and therefore the responsibility of a site or branch manager. For companies to obtain the best value for their efforts on behalf of the community, it is essential that local management decisions should be made within the context of a well-defined company policy.

The lead has to come from the top and it is for the chairman and the board to draw up the company's community affairs policy and to communicate it throughout the enterprise. They also have to ensure that there is an organisational structure in place for putting the policy into effect. Unless this is done, the response to the policy will depend on the public-spiritedness of individual managers and there will be no reliable means of monitoring its progress or of modifying it in the light of experience.

Guidelines

What criteria might boards use to decide on the level of support to put behind their companies' social objectives? The main resources which companies have to offer to the community are people and money; on the whole, management skills are in even shorter supply in the social field than funds. Loaning experienced and committed managers to the community can achieve what donations of cash on their own cannot.

As to the scale on which companies might invest in the society from which they draw their livelihood, Lord Laing, when he was chairman of United Biscuits, set standards which represent current best practice. He founded the Per Cent Club in 1986 and companies joining the Club agree to give the equivalent of 0.5 per cent of their United Kingdom pre-tax profits to support community projects in Britain. The aim is to lift the target from 0.5 per cent to 1 per cent over time. That figure includes both cash donations and the value of second-ments. On secondments, United Biscuits has worked broadly on the basis of having one person on secondment for every 2,000 employees. These levels of support set by a leading company provide chairmen with some useful benchmarks.

Community affairs budget

The way in which a board allocates its company's community affairs budget is a matter of individual choice. It may, however, be helpful to say something about the way in which Cadbury Schweppes approached the matter, simply as an illustration.

The board began by defining the kinds of community activity which it thought the company should support. The first test was that the organisations concerned should be working in fields which were relevant to the company's long-term strategic objectives. Within that category, a further test was the degree of common interest between the aims of the organisation and those of the company. In addition to common aims, the board was also looking for shared values, for bodies which had the same kind of outlook as the company on people and on priorities. Two further points to be taken into account were the capacity of the organisations concerned to become self-sustaining and the closeness of their links with any of the company's sites.

The company also gave its support to Business in the Community, an organisation set up and funded by companies to put new heart into Britain's older industrial areas. They did this on the basis that many community problems were best tackled by companies working together in a co-ordinated way, rather than on their own. By working through a collective body, like Business in the Community, companies encourage others to join it. One of the ways in which established companies can help new local initiatives is by backing them at a formative stage and thereby giving them their seal of approval.

In dealing with charitable appeals, the company worked to six main headings, between which a rough split of the charitable budget had been agreed in advance. The headings were as follows:

- job creation and youth employment;
- environment;
- education/business links;
- health and welfare;
- clubs and societies in local communities;
- industry-related causes.

Other companies would choose different headings and allocate their funds in different proportions between them. The main point is that by having clear guidelines, the difficult task of discriminating between the many worthy causes which come across the chairman's desk is made manageable. A clear policy focus means that the company's support is targeted and therefore more effective than if it were spread thinner and more widely. It also enables a brief statement of the company's policy to be sent to those whose appeals fall outside the guidelines.

Two more general points concern the support which companies give to the community in terms of the time of their employees and the backing which companies can give to the voluntary efforts of employees.

Backing the efforts of employees

On the first point, secondments come naturally to mind when thinking of ways in which companies can help the community through people. Secondments are indeed invaluable and can achieve what part-time help cannot. But the sheer scale of the part-time help which people from business give to the community is impressive. Some of it is in working hours, most of it is not. By sitting on a school governing body, by being a committee member of a voluntary organisation or by belonging to one, employees are putting business experience to work in the community. Most of this volunteer help will be the result of individual initiative, rather than being organised through the company. Where the company can play its part is by letting employees know what kind of help is needed by local organisations and by making it as easy as possible for employees to serve the community in this way.

On the second point, there are two useful means of backing the voluntary efforts of employees. One is to regard the active involvement of employees in a cause as a strong argument for giving it company support. The other is for the company to match charitable donations made by its employees. This ensures that the company's contributions go to causes which the work-force has identified as worthwhile; it also helps to raise the level of charitable giving in general.

JOBS

Decisions on which community activities a company should support and the extent to which it should support them are not the sum of a company's social policy. It also has judgements to make in the middle ground between its inward responsibilities to the business and its outward responsibilities to society. The decisions which face a company when it introduces new technology or concentrates its production facilities, are examples of this kind of issue. They are business decisions with social implications. The immediate effect of investing in automation or of closing a factory will be to reduce employment. What responsibilities do companies, taking such actions, have to the community over the provision of jobs?

The primary aim

The starting-point has to be the primary aim of companies, which is to meet the needs of their customers for goods and services. Everyone is a consumer; some consumers are employees. Satisfying customers requires companies to compete in the market-place; they cannot therefore opt out of introducing new technology in order to preserve jobs. To do so would be to deny consumers the benefits of technical progress, to short-change the shareholders and, in the longer run, to put the jobs of everyone in the company at risk. What destroys jobs certainly and permanently is the failure to be competitive.

The record of experience is that technological progress creates more jobs than it eliminates, in ways which cannot be forecast. It may do so, however, only after a time-lag and those displaced may not, through lack of skills, be able to take advantage of the new opportunities when they arise. Nevertheless, the company's prime responsibility to everyone who has a stake in it is to retain its competitive edge, even if this means a loss of jobs in the short run.

Management of change

Where the company does have a responsibility to society is in the manner in which it manages change. This includes the need to foresee and plan the introduction of new technology, at the same time involving those who will be affected by it in the way in which it is to be introduced. The longer the notice of changes resulting in a loss of jobs, the better the chances of using natural wastage or early retirement to close the gap and the greater the likelihood of those who will lose out being able to find alternative employment. If the reduction by one company in its work-force hits a particular area, then the company can take steps to encourage new businesses to start up in the locality; British Steel, British Coal and Pilkington have demonstrated in Britain what it is possible to do through successful initiatives of this kind.

Companies also possess a vital resource, from the community's point of view, which is their capacity to provide training. The provision of appropriate training enables continuing employees to take advantage of change and those who lose their jobs as a result of it to find new ones more readily.

Companies cannot set out to create jobs as a goal. Their task is to meet the needs of their customers; if they do that successfully, the jobs will follow. What they can do, however, is to support organisations like Business in the Community and local enterprise agencies, which have been set up to encourage the formation of new enterprises. In this way, companies are able to create employment collectively, even if they are unable to do so individually.

Benefits of change

It is easier for boards to see the need for change and its ultimate benefits, than it is for most other groups in society, including politicians, administrators and those belonging to the professions. Companies earn their living in markets which are forever changing. Their continued existence depends on their ability to read the signs of change correctly and to make the most of the opportunities that change presents. Society, on the other hand, has a literally vested interest in preserving the present structure, whether it be of industry or of jobs. This is why the balance on this issue of jobs now, versus jobs in the future, is difficult to strike in a way which society in general will see as socially responsible.

Need for decisions

The last point I want to make in this section is to draw attention to the pressures on boards not to put through programmes of change which will have repercussions on the community. It is the job of chairmen and their boards to see that companies face up to the difficult choices which confront them and to implement such changes as are necessary promptly and efficiently and with due regard to their consequences for people. What is a matter for concern is when public pressure – no doubt well intentioned – is brought to bear on companies in the name of social responsibility to put off such disagreeable decisions as the closure of uneconomic plants.

The board which takes drastic action in order that its company should survive is more likely to be criticised publicly than the board which fails to grasp the nettle and whose business gradually, but inexorably, declines. There is always a temptation in business to postpone difficult decisions, but it is not in society's interests that hard choices should be evaded because of public clamour. True social responsibility requires that chairmen and boards should be encouraged to take the decisions facing their companies, however thorny. The responsibility for providing that encouragement rests with society as a whole.

THE BUSINESS RECORD ON SOCIAL RESPONSIBILITY

By way of conclusion, what has been the record of British companies to date in carrying out their responsibilities to the community? I would suggest that the main failure of business has been its slowness to pick up society's signals and to see the direction in which companies were bound to move. Over such issues as pollution or consumerism, the first reaction of business has been one of opposition. As a consequence of taking up this position, later attempts to modify proposals for controls in a practical way have been seen as a change of tactics, not of heart. In other instances, companies have lain low and hoped that the pressures for action would prove ephemeral. The lesson is that companies should pay attention to forecasting social changes in the same way as they do changes in their markets. This will guide them as to which social trends are relevant to their type of business and help them to identify appropriate social objectives; these may well be different from the ones which are being pressed on them most stridently.

Openness

Companies have to pick up the signals as to the pace and direction of society's expectations of business, so that they can play an active part in shaping the new rules, whether statutory or voluntary, within which they will have to work. A readiness by companies to provide more information about their policies and actions in fields of social concern is an important element in encouraging this dialogue. Disclosure is not in itself a panacea for improving the relationship between business and society, but it represents a willingness to operate an open system which is the foundation of that relationship. Companies need to be open to the views of society and open in return about their own activities. This is a necessary condition for the establishment of trust and for the sensible resolution of conflicts of interest.

The political process

Companies then have to be prepared to become more involved in the political process through which governments respond to social pressures, so that they can play their part in that process more effectively. Companies have to learn how to combine serving their customers in the market-place and the social interest in the political forum. One way of doing so is to encourage employees at all levels to play their full part in social and political affairs. Not only will they have a valuable contribution to make, based on practical experience, but they will also become more aware of the trend of social aims and more alert to society's expectations of business.

Secondments

One means for companies to advance the social cause is for them to second able managers to community organisations. The ability to manage is a rare resource and the lack of management experience is at least as much of a handicap to most social institutions as is the lack of money. Successful secondments benefit everyone concerned: the giving and receiving institutions and the individual secondees. The best work of reference on secondments which I have come across is the one published by IBM describing the secondment policies and practices of their United Kingdom company (Peach 1983).

Reasons for involvement

The loan of managerial talent to help to achieve community goals is a working example of the way in which business and society interact. Companies are part of society and their ability to achieve their business aims depends on the health of the society in which they operate. By contributing to the solution of some of society's most pressing problems, companies improve their own environment and therefore their own chances of success.

The defensive argument to the same end is that failure by business to keep in touch with society's views of its responsibilities will lead to increasing regulation, with all its attendant inefficiencies. Alternatively, society will attempt to reduce the power of business if it thinks that power is being used to the detriment of the community. What Keith Davis referred to in 1975 as 'the iron law of responsibility' states: 'In the long run those who do not use power in a manner which society considers responsible will tend to lose it.'

Finally, an important positive reason for companies to be seen to be meeting society's expectations of them is the vital need to attract able young people into industry and commerce. This is essential for companies and for society if scarce resources are to be used effectively and the social aims of the community and of business are to be financed. Companies will win the commitment of people of the calibre they need, only if they are seen to be making a worthwhile contribution to society.

CHAPTER 10

THE CHAIRMAN'S ROLE IN PERSPECTIVE

This chapter deals with matters which are not so directly related to the chairman's responsibilities for the work of the board as those which have preceded it. They are, nevertheless, important since they include the appointment and removal of chairmen, the balance between the task of chairmen as chairmen and their other activities, the chairmanship of subsidiary boards, the chairman's position in a take-over and the role of the chairman in relation to a company's values.

APPOINTMENT OF THE CHAIRMAN

It seems logical to begin with the way in which chairmen find themselves in the chair. I have referred throughout to chairmen being appointed by their board colleagues and that is how it should be. It is the duty of retiring chairmen to ensure that there is an orderly handover to their successors and that their successors have the support of their boards. There is, however, anecdotal evidence to the effect that the succession process is not always well managed and that chairmen have been appointed because it had been generally accepted that they would inherit the chair, or simply because they seemed to be the best available candidate on the board at the time. Certainly, I have known of a board where more than one of the outside directors were under the impression that they had been invited on the board to succeed the chairman.

The starting-point is that chairmen should have terms of office and some understanding with their boards about the age at which they retire. This sets the timetable for finding a successor. Assuming that the board has outside, independent directors on it (and sorting out the succession is clearly a more difficult matter with a wholly executive board) then the chairman will talk with them individually and collectively about the options.

Taking the straightforward situation where there is both a chairman and a chief executive, and only the chairman is retiring, there will be three options. One is to appoint an existing board member, the second is to recruit a new board member as the potential chairman and the third would be to combine the two top jobs, making the chief executive the chairman's successor.

Inside and outside candidates

The main issue is whether to appoint from within or to bring in someone from outside the company. In the Heidrick and Struggles' survey, referred to in the first chapter, there was an even division between chairmen who had been appointed from within their own companies and those who came from outside. The arguments for looking outside the company, as well as within it, and for enlisting the help of professional agencies in the search, is that this is a crucially important decision for a board. The board should not simply be concerned to find a chairman, but to find the best chairman that it can. The only way in which the board can assess the calibre of the inside candidates is by comparing them with those who might be brought in from outside the company.

Appointment procedure

I would expect chairmen, in the first instance, to sound out their outside directors on whether or not to look for their successors beyond the existing board membership. Having established where the independent directors stand, they would seek support for their approach from the executive directors individually. It is the chairman's job to see that, however the appointment is made, it has board support. To bring a new outside director onto the board as the chairman's successor, when the executive directors favoured an existing board member, would divide the board. Equally, anyone joining a board in the expectation of succeeding the chairman will want to be assured that the proposal is backed by the board, and it is only the chairman who can give that assurance.

If a new appointment is to be made to a board, with a view to the person concerned taking over from the chairman, then that is probably the best way of expressing the position. By that, I mean that the new director has joined the board in the expectation, both of the board and of the individual, of being elected chairman when the time comes. This still leaves the final decision with the board, where it belongs. While it would clearly be difficult for the board to make a different appointment when the time came, it would be possible for them to do so. Such a decision would be embarrassing for the chairman-designate, but it would be preferable to having the title of chairman without the full backing and, therefore, authority of the board.

What manner of chairman?

The underlying issue for a board, in coming to a conclusion about the chairmanship, is what kind of chairman are they looking for. One element of choice is between a chairman who will broadly maintain the company on its existing course and one who is likely to feel that a change, either of direction or of pace, is needed. The labels 'conservative' and 'radical' have perhaps too many political overtones to describe at all accurately the choices a board has in this matter; they may unintentionally belittle the importance, at certain stages in a company's development, of consolidating what has gone before. Conservation does not mean inaction, since it requires the organisation to maintain its capacity to progress through investing in its human and physical resources. Nevertheless, the first divide is between a conservative chairman, who will aim to keep the company on its present lines, and a radical chairman, whose instinct will be to bring about change.

The other divide is one of style – and styles of leadership vary considerably from the autocratic to the participative. The personal styles of chairmen also vary. There are those who lead from the front by force of personality and there are those who fit the classical description of leadership – 'He that governs sits quietly at the stern and scarce is seen to stir.' Individuals have to discover for themselves their natural style of leadership and then develop it. The straightforward point is that a particular kind of chairman will suit a particular board at a particular time.

Boards, therefore, need to decide what it is that they expect of their chairmen and what type of chairman best fits their needs. The clearer the picture that they have of their prospective chairman, the more likely it is that they will make a successful appointment.

In drawing up their specification for a chairman, boards will have two points in mind. One is the likely span of the chairman's appointment. The board has to assess not only what manner of chairman their situation demands today, but what it is likely to demand during the chairman's tenure of office. The second point is that chairmen are entitled to assume that their appointment was made after due analysis and that it was a deliberate decision whose consequences were anticipated. That was my view on being first appointed as chairman of a board. I had not expected to be appointed and I took the decision as a vote in favour of breaking with the past.

DROPPING THE PILOT

So much for the appointment of the chairman; but there will also be occasions for parting, when the board decides either that their vision of the future of the company has diverged from that of their chairman, or that their chairman's style no longer meets the needs of the situation. There is no generally established constitutional way of bringing about a change of chairman, since someone other than the chairman has to call a board meeting from which the chairman, although a board member, would be excluded. While it is true to say that the law and a company's articles accord the position of chairman to whoever is elected to the chair at any particular gathering of board members, the decision to bring about a formal change of chairmanship is not just a domestic matter for the board; it has wider implications in line with the increased recognition which the post has acquired.

Change from within

If the move to bring about a change comes from within the company, dissatisfied board members would probably approach the deputy chairman or the chief executive and ask one of them to take the initiative in consulting all the other board members and then telling the chairman that the board no longer had confidence in their leadership. The problem would be to avoid an atmosphere of conspiracy, which, combined with a period of uncertainty while board members were making up their minds whether or not to act, could be damaging to the company.

When Cecil King, who chaired the International Publishing Corporation up to 1968, was deposed as chairman, it is said that his butler brought him a note from the remainder of his board while he was shaving, informing him that he had been replaced. It was an example which left all chairmen slightly uneasier in their positions than before, especially on getting up in the morning. Perhaps all that can usefully be said on the possible need to replace a chairman is that it reinforces the argument for limited terms of office and that if it has to be done, let it be done speedily.

Change from without

It may be, however, that the pressure to replace the chairman comes not from within the board, but externally from the shareholders. This pressure may be applied privately or publicly. A private approach could be made by one or more major institutional shareholders to influential members of the board, in order to persuade them that change was needed.

Assuming that their arguments were successful, the main body of board members would arrange for the resignation or retirement of the chairman and for the appointment of someone in their place, who better met the needs of the board and of the shareholders. Bringing about change at the top in this way seems to me to be an unimpeachable example of the institutions using their power in the interests of all the shareholders and of the company. The acceptance by the institutions of that degree of responsibility for the governance of the companies in which they have invested, is much to be encouraged.

A more contentious means to the same end comes about when the pressure for the chairman to stand down is brought to bear publicly. A recent press report describing just such a situation ran as follows:

> Institutional shareholders are sounding out those who support the move and are confident that they can muster the numbers. They will shortly present the chairman with a fait accompli – that he either resigns or they will call an extraordinary general meeting and vote that he be removed from the board.

That describes a method by which shareholders can bring about change through a general meeting. But it is change in response to a crisis and it risks forcing the resignation issue through, without proper time for reflection or for a thorough search for the best available successor. Private pressure is likely to lead to a better outcome in the longer term than public clamour. If there was more of the former, there would be less cause for the latter.

Be that as it may, chairmen presented with this kind of ultimatum, backed by the shareholders, have little option but to resign. While this may be in line with their duty to the company, they will also have regard to their duty not to leave the board in disarray at a time of difficulty. This may involve riding out the storm, until a suitable replacement can be found who commands the confidence of the shareholders and the board.

The Guinness approach

Guinness plc is an example of a company which, unusually, has included in its Articles of Association formal arrangements for the election and removal of their chairman. The Guinness board is required, under its Articles, to establish a Non-Executive Committee made up of all board members save those appointed as executive directors. The relevant Article sets out the Committee's remit as follows:

> The Non-Executive Committee shall have the sole power to elect the chairman and any vice-chairman or vice-chairmen and any deputy chairman or deputy chairmen of the Board with the power to remove any person so appointed, the power to determine the period for which and the basis on which chairman, vice-chairman or vice-chairmen or deputy chairman or deputy chairmen holds office.

As a result, the Guinness board has an overt and orderly process for appointing or removing its chairman; an example which deserves to be followed. In more general terms, the appointment of the Non-Executive Committee was part of the board's system of checks and balances. Guinness had, at the time, an executive chairman who effectively combined the posts of chairman and chief executive. The basis for this arrangement was that the chairman had two managing directors, each in charge of one of the company's two core businesses, reporting to him. There was, therefore, a division of responsibilities at the head of the company. The executive chairman was nevertheless in a powerful position, being responsible both for the board and for the management of the enterprise. This made it prudent for the board to build appropriate checks and balances into its governance structure.

Thus the Non-Executive Committee was formed to strengthen the position of the outside directors, and thereby of the board, in relation to the chairman. It acknowledged the role of the outside directors in the election and dismissal of the chairman and made clear how, and by whom, these crucial decisions were to be made. The Guinness example also illustrates that companies have to shape their own patterns of governance, in the light of the particular needs of their boards and shareholders.

THE CHAIRMAN'S RANGE OF ACTIVITIES

One reason why chairmen could lose the confidence of their boards is through taking on too many other duties. This raises the question of how far the activities of chairmen outside their companies can assist them in their chairmanship.

In the usual division of work between chairmen and chief executives, the chairman looks outwards to the external constituencies of the company and also stands further back from the workings of the company than the chief executive. This degree of detachment is an asset to chairmen in maintaining their focus on the work of the board, rather than on the cut and thrust of operations, and in keeping strategy and the future of the business in the forefront of their minds.

Such an approach does not imply any lack of commitment to the enterprise, but it enables chairmen to analyse the business scene as a whole and to do so reasonably objectively. It means that the chairman can come to a judgement on an issue facing the company, without being unduly constrained by the received wisdom with which most businesses are well endowed. A certain independence of thought is a valuable attribute for a chairman, but how can that independence best be developed?

The transfer of experience

Its main source is experience beyond the company. When chairmen are involved in activities outside their businesses, they are engaged in transferring what they have learnt from their own enterprises into those outside activities and vice versa. They can check that the decisions being made in both spheres reflect a common view of the way in which the world is moving and of the way in which people behave. If they do not, chairmen will analyse why the discrepancy has occurred and question which of their sources of experience seems to be out of line.

Because the problems and choices confronting their companies are in chairmen's minds, they file away information which they pick up elsewhere and which could have a bearing on their main businesses. In the same way, they will be exchanging ideas between their different interests and activities. As Alfred Sloan wrote in *My Years with General Motors*, the best of books on organising a company: 'There is a logical way of doing business in accordance with the facts and circumstances of an industry, if you can figure it out.'

It is the figuring out that is the challenge and the more contact chairmen have with the world outside their companies, the better their figuring is likely to be. What does this suggest in terms of the relationship between the job of chairmen as chairmen and any other interests which they may wish to pursue?

The relationship between inside and outside activities

We are back to balance again, and the first factor to be considered is how much time the chairmanship demands. Clearly the chairman's job as chairman has first call not only on their time, but on how it is distributed. A handful of chairmen would argue that their duty to their company debars them from undertaking any other significant responsibilities. Most would find this too rigorous a stance, since it would mean that their inspiration could only come from their main job or from their leisure interests.

There are, perhaps, four main fields of activity open to chairmen, in addition to their task as chairmen. They are other chairmanships or directorships, serving on bodies which are associated with business, public service in various forms and the whole range of other activities, from charitable work to how they use their spare time. All four can have a part to play as sources for ideas, which either are directly relevant to their companies or which help chairmen to see business problems in a new light. They also have a part to play in keeping chairmen sound of body and mind. Although the four headings are listed in order of the closeness of their relationship to the business world, this does not imply that holding an outside directorship is necessarily of greater value than any other kind of external involvement.

Membership of boards

Nevertheless, I feel that as chairman I gained most benefit from being a member of the board of another company in an entirely different field. I was clear, however, in terms of the balance of time, that I could not sit on more than two outside boards if I was to be able to give the necessary attention to their affairs and to those of the company of which I was chairman. The practical advantage of being on boards other than your own is that you learn directly from them, largely to the extent to which you contribute to them.

Business organisations

The second category of business-related bodies covers a number of different types of organisation. To start with, there are industry and trade associations. I have been involved with such industry-wide associations as the Confederation of British Industry and the Chambers of Industry and Commerce and also with the associations representing the interests of the food industry in Britain, in the European Union and in the United States.

Organisations such as the CBI offer the opportunity to become involved in the ways in which business policy is formed and in which business influences political opinion. It has to be useful to chairmen to have some understanding of how to translate business points of view into political action. Another advantage of taking part in an organisation which represents business on national and international issues is that it opens up new networks of contacts. It provides a structure within which personal links can be formed through working with individuals, as opposed simply to meeting them. Industry-wide bodies can, therefore, provide an insight into the political process, an opportunity to have a hand in formulating policies and the chance to work with a cross-section of people in the public and private sectors.

Representing the company's interests on a trade or professional association offers more limited openings into the wider world. The argument for spending time on this kind of work is based on ensuring that the company's interests are effectively represented, rather than their being represented by those whose time the company can most easily spare. Trade association representation is an investment by the company, and by the individual concerned, in safeguarding the interests of the company, and it is an expression of the company's duty to its industry.

Public service

Duty to the industry leads on to public duty and to service on government commissions, local authority bodies and so on. Again, there is much to be gained from a first-hand understanding of the workings of institutions outside the private sector. The experience of serving on an official commission of inquiry will have something of value to offer to chairmen in their work and will put them in touch with people whom they would be unlikely to come across in the world of business. Nevertheless, a sense of duty will be the main reason for chairmen undertaking public work.

The final heading covers everything else, such as charitable, political or educational activities. All are ways of putting business experience to social use and will be not without benefit to the company.

Advantages of outside activities

Basis of independence

There are a number of general points to be made about the advantages of chairmen undertaking activities removed from the company. One is that it prevents chairmen becoming too inward-looking. Their positions outside the company give them an external standpoint from which to judge the issues arising within their businesses. Outside posts confer on them a degree of independence, in the literal sense, because they are not then wholly dependent on the ways of thinking of the companies whose boards they chair. The independence of outlook required of a chairman is not a passive quality derived from not being wholly involved in the company's affairs. Effective independence is established through knowledge and experience acquired in other companies and other fields. They give chairmen confidence in their own judgement through knowing that their standards and their approach to their tasks are broadly based.

Source of innovation

The second point is that the chairman's role as initiator is greatly assisted by having access to sources of innovative thinking, not just outside the company, but possibly quite unrelated to business at all. In theory, there are unlimited opportunities to pick up ideas on management through reading books and articles. Interestingly, most people in business fall into two distinct groups over management literature: some can never bring themselves to open a book on business, others read them avidly – especially on aeroplanes. That aside, having responsibilities unconnected with the company provides chairmen with first-hand experience of the way in which ideas are applied in other contexts. This is of much greater practical value than simply culling ideas from a variety of sources. What is useful to chairmen is to see new concepts put into practice in other organisations, and this can only come from being directly involved in their activities.

Personal contacts

The same kind of reasoning applies to the next point, which concerns the personal contacts built up by chairmen through their interests outside the company. Social links can be useful, but the links which are formed through working with people to achieve a common purpose are stronger. I mentioned in an earlier chapter that it was helpful if a chairman had contacts with those in Parliament and the Civil Service who had an interest in the company's affairs. Chairmen who have worked alongside civil servants or members of Parliament will know how their minds work, as well as how the apparatus of government functions. Should the company want to put its case to government, it can find out to whom to write from Vacher's *Parliamentary Companion*, but how to write and how to follow up the letter needs to be based on a working knowledge of the political system and of those who operate it.

Experience of chairmanship

Another relevant point is that any of these external activities, from serving on the board of another company to assisting in some charitable endeavour, may provide the opportunity to take the chair, or indeed may provide no escape from so doing. Wider experience of chairmanship can only be of value to chairmen and their boards. In the same way, serving on other bodies may offer the opportunity, as it did for me, of learning from their chairmen.

As a last word on this subject, the relationship between a chairman's task as chairman and everything else that they may undertake comes back to questions of balance and of individual inclination. The position in the company for which I believe it is especially important to have outside points of reference to work to, is that of chairman. Every chairman will have their own view on how such points of reference can most appropriately be established.

SUBSIDIARY BOARDS

The next point for discussion is what the differences are between chairing the main board of a company and the board of one of its subsidiaries. I was for some years a member of a subsidiary board of an American company and when I was chairman of a public company, I worked closely with the chairmen of companies within our group in which the parent company held all, a majority or a minority of the shares. On the basis of that experience, I believe that there are issues of special relevance to the chairing of boards of subsidiary companies.

Wholly-owned subsidiaries

If the subsidiaries are wholly-owned, the position of the chairmen of their boards is reasonably straightforward. They are broadly in the same position as the chairmen of boards of operating divisions of a large company. The task of such a board is to direct the affairs of the subsidiary or the division in the interests of the parent company. In doing so, however, their chairmen will have two aims in mind.

The first will be to encourage the board to think and act like a board and not like a management committee. This is made easier if the subsidiary board has outside directors on it, and it is possible to make such appointments to divisional boards, as well as to wholly-owned subsidiary boards. In fact, divisional boards present companies with the opportunity to offer terms of office on them to able candidates from the public sector. This kind of interchange is valuable to both parties; the problem with making public-sector appointments to the main boards of companies is the possibility that conflicts of interest will at some stage arise. This is less likely to be an issue at the level of a divisional board.

The chairman's second aim will be to handle constructively the tensions which will inevitably arise between the views of the subsidiary board and those of the parent board. They will arise from the subsidiary board acting as a board in its own right and promoting the interests of its division of the company. The more successful chairmen are in getting their boards to work as boards, the more likely it is that they will not see eye to eye with their parent company, and it is the chairman who will have to bridge the gap between the two boards.

One reason for forming boards of this kind can be to train the executives on them in the workings of boards. If training is the objective, it is essential that the chairman encourages board members to take their decisions as directors and not as managers. This will add to the tensions between the subsidiary and the parent, but it is all part of learning the difference between being a director and a manager.

Partially-owned subsidiaries

The more usual situation, however, is when the subsidiary is not wholly-owned, but has other shareholders whose interests need to be taken into account. Such shareholdings can arise for a number of reasons, such as the requirement in some countries to have local partners or because the original owners of an acquisition wish to retain a stake. Whether the parent company owns a majority or a minority holding affects the relationship between the two companies, but it does not alter the chairman's constitutional position.

The job of the board of a subsidiary company is to act in the best interests of that company, since it is to the company that the board members owe their duty. The chairman has to ensure that the board is not influenced by any one set of shareholder interests to act in a way which might be held to be contrary to the interests of the company – for example, by paying a larger dividend than was consistent with a sound policy of reinvestment, in order to meet the main shareholder's need for cash. The test which the chairman and the board have to apply is whether they would have taken the same decision had the company been independent.

Overseas subsidiaries

The potential conflicts of interest between parent companies and their subsidiaries probably arise most acutely when the subsidiary is in an overseas territory, whose nationals hold shares in it. For example, a British company may be the majority shareholder in an overseas business, with the remaining shares widely held by the local community. It is likely in that situation that the chairman and the majority of the board members will be citizens of the country concerned, as will most of the managers.

Such a subsidiary company might then be urged by government officials to diversify into a line of business to which the government accorded a high priority, but of which the parent company had no experience. The pressures on the chairman and the board to fall in with the government's wishes would be likely to be considerable in this event and inevitably the views of local board members, shareholders and managers would be more immediate and insistent than those of the distant parent company. The parent in its turn, even if it had a majority, will be cautious about using its voting power to override the views of its board members on the spot, on whom it would rely for advice as to how to act as a good corporate citizen in the local context.

In handling this kind of conflict, the lead given by the chairman is crucial. Chairmen have to be able to retain the confidence of their own boards and that of their parent companies. They have to be prepared to stand up to pressures from their local shareholders and, if need be, from their main shareholder. Maintaining the confidence of all the interests involved will almost certainly impose a considerable burden of travelling. It is only by building up good personal contacts with the appropriate people in the parent company that chairmen of subsidiaries can earn their trust and enable them to understand the local point of view.

From the parent company's standpoint, the appointment of the chairman of the board of an overseas subsidiary is crucial. Equally, the local board has to accept that, for the relationship between the parent and the subsidiary to work, the chairman has to be someone who can lead and who will command the respect of all shareholders. The chairmen of such boards, therefore, have to recognise that their job is potentially more difficult than if their companies were independent. Their touchstone has to remain the best interests of the company whose board they chair, even if that is not always appreciated by their local shareholders or by the parent company. Chairmen act as the link, and the relationship between parent companies and their subsidiary boards largely depends on them.

CHAIRMEN AND TAKEOVERS

A matter which is never far from the minds of the chairmen of boards of most quoted companies is whether they will find themselves defending their company from being taken over. Bids and takeovers raise a raft of important issues which are outside our scope, but they also put more responsibility on the chairman than any other event this side of bankruptcy. The reason why defending a contested bid lays such a burden on the chairman is because of the conflicts of interest which a bid can generate. Oversimplifying the situation considerably, the key interests to be taken into account are those of the shareholders and those of the employees, which may in turn subdivide into the interests of the executive directors and senior managers and the interests of the employees in general.

Since the executive members of the board have a career interest in the outcome of a bid, the chairman has to be especially vigilant in ensuring that the board holds a proper balance between the interests of the shareholders and those of the employees. There can be no more demanding test of chairmanship. Difficult matters of business judgement are involved, to which are added strong emotions, extreme pressures of time and perhaps the glare of publicity as well. What can usefully be said about the chairman's responsibilities when faced with all the conflicts associated with a bid?

Bid responsibilities of chairmen

One of the chairman's responsibilities is to see that a bid does not take the board and the company by surprise. Boards which consider that their companies are potential targets will, no doubt, have appointed a defence team, probably headed by the finance director. The team will have prepared a basic defence document and will have all the external professional links already in place. This is one pillar of defence; the other is the support of the shareholders, which, in turn, will depend on the relationships built up over time by the chairman and the senior executives with their shareholders.

Establishing the right kind of relationship with the shareholders is like growing asparagus – you need to have started three years ago. It will have been up to the chairman and the board to have kept the shareholders informed about the progress of the business and their plans for its future development. If the board are looking to the loyalty of their investors when a bid comes, they need to have earned it by having already set up regular channels of communication with their shareholders.

The chairman's responsibility once the bid has been launched is to lead the defence. The fact that there is a bid presumes that the bidder either failed to reach agreement with the board or did not believe agreement to be possible. A bid is a move to force the board's hand and the board's first reaction will be to turn it down. At this stage, the chairman is likely to be on safe ground in believing that the interests, both of the shareholders and of the employees, can best be served through the company retaining its independence or finding an alliance of its own choice.

Need for independent judgement

It is when the bidding company either stands firm on its initial offer, or raises it, that chairmen have to exercise their independent judgement, along with their outside directors. In terms of the value which the bid places on the company, the board has to weigh the bid offer against what it can realistically expect to achieve for the shareholders itself. This requires considerable judgement, given that the offer price will be firm, while the board's forecast of the future earning power of the company can only be an estimate.

Interests of employees

Where the interests of the employees lie will depend on the intentions of both the bidders and the defenders. By which I mean that the figures put forward by either side will be justified on the grounds of the actions to be taken to live up to them – selling parts of the business, closing factories, reducing labour and so on. The higher the price, the more drastic the action which may have to be taken by whoever ultimately controls the company. The board, therefore, needs to take account of the implications for the employees of their defensive tactics.

The Rowntree example

A practical example of how it is possible to balance the interests of shareholders, employees and, in this case, those of the local community in defending against a bid was provided in 1988 by the Rowntree company. Nestlé and Jacobs Suchard both acquired 29.9 per cent stakes in Rowntree and both launched bids for the business. The Rowntree board negotiated the highest price they could for their company from Nestlé, thus meeting their responsibilities to their shareholders.

However, they negotiated about the future conduct of the business at the same time and arrived at a total package, which they judged best met the interests of all those who would be affected by their loss of independence. They gained assurances about employment prospects and about the role of their head office at York, which was to take over responsibility for Nestlé's confectionery strategy worldwide as part of the bargain. In particular, the board received undertakings that Rowntree's policies towards its own work-force and towards its relationship with the community would continue.

Responsibilities to the executives

One further area of responsibility for chairmen is to safeguard, as far as possible, the executives of their company against retribution for the vigour of their defence, should the bid succeed. This is where their leadership of the defence is important, if the bid has been hotly contested. It is then the chairman who forced the price up against the bidder, rather than the executives, whose careers will be at stake if their company is taken over.

Considerations of structure

Two final points are worth making. The first is the advantage, in this context, of having both a chairman and a chief executive, when a company is faced with a bid. The person who is both chairman and chief executive is more likely to feel vulnerable to the charge of favouring the interests of management as against those of the shareholders; equally, their position is not as independent as that of a chairman in resolving conflicts of interest.

The second point concerns the key role which outside directors can play, because of their independence, on the boards of both bidding and defending companies. The advantages of having disinterested, independent directors on either side in a bid have been cogently argued by Lord Rees-Mogg, in an article in *The Independent*, on 12 September 1989. His article was entitled 'The value of an outside voice in the drama of a takeover bid' and was based on his experience as an outside director of both bidding and defending companies.

A COMPANY'S VALUES

The final aspect of the chairman's role which I want to pick up in this chapter, is that of guardian of the company's values. The ultimate responsibility for actions carried out in the name of the company rests with the chairman. Chairmen, therefore, need to be aware of what the people who make up their companies believe is expected of them. They will also be concerned to ensure that the values for which their companies stand are maintained.

A good deal has been written about the so-called 'cultures' of companies. I welcome the recognition which has thus been given to an important element of company life, although I do not think that the word 'culture' is particularly appropriate. The basic meaning of culture as defined in the dictionary is: 'the training and refinement of mind, tastes and manners'. If that definition is applied to companies it carries with it the suggestion that culture is a result of training and that, therefore, it can be changed in a desired direction through the refining process.

The character of a company

This is altogether too superficial a view of what I prefer to call the character of a company. All groups evolve an identity over time and develop their own codes of conduct and systems of values. That identity and the unwritten rules which sum up the way in which things are done in a company add up to its character. Every company has its own character, some more distinctive than others. The reason why I doubt if the character of a company can be changed at will is that it is an amalgam of the beliefs and attitudes of everyone who is part of the enterprise.

If the company's character is formed from within, then this limits the ability of chairmen to bring about changes in it – except for the worse, if they were to set a bad example from the top. While the chairman's influence may be limited, it is nevertheless important. In the first place, aspects of a company's character can be changed, provided all concerned can be brought to see the need for change. It is possible, for example, for the chairman and the board to encourage a shift from a conformist attitude to a questioning one. A shift of that kind does not alter the basic values of the company, but it will change behaviour. Similarly, concern for quality or for customer service can be heightened. The stronger the degree of trust in the leadership, the more possible it is to bring about changes of that kind.

Establishment of values

A further compelling reason why the character of their companies should be a matter of concern for chairmen is that, without a clear lead from them and their boards, there may be confusion down the line as to what their real values are. A stark example of what can go wrong, if the leader's trumpet gives an uncertain sound, is to be found in the case study of the actions brought against General Electric in the United States for price-fixing in 1960. The whole sad story was documented in *The Fate of the Edsel and Other Business Adventures*, by John Brooks, which came out in 1964.

Confusion at General Electric

The point at issue was that the board of General Electric had laid down rules which forbade the practice of discussing prices with competitors. But the executives down the line were unsure whether the board really meant what it said. The way they overcame this uncertainty over the message from on high, was to see whether or not it was accompanied by a wink. If the executive who told them not to break the law was thought to have winked while doing so, the order was disregarded.

This led to executives being characterised as 'winkers' or 'anti-winkers', all of which sounds absurd, but the penalty for the absurdity was that some senior executives were sent to jail for their part in the affair. What caused their downfall was muddle and uncertainty. The muddle probably arose because the signals from the top were contradictory, with the managers being told to keep within the law but also to achieve their profit targets. They could then be in doubt over what priority to give to those two orders.

The lesson is clear: the chairman and the board not only have to establish the company's standards of behaviour, but they have to see that they are communicated throughout the organisation and that the company's reward system reinforces them.

Company principles

In my judgement, it is helpful for chairmen to commit to writing what they believe their companies stand for. This is hard to do, because such statements are apt to seem platitudinous to their authors, but that is not how they will seem to others in the company, especially those who are furthest from headquarters. I have included as Appendix 1 a statement, which I wrote as chairman, called 'The Character of the Company'. It represented my view at the time of the kind of company we were and of the kind of company we should aim to become. The point about time is important, because any such statement should be open to rewriting, in whole or in part, as circumstances change. Its purpose is not to act as a brake on change, but to encourage change in the right direction.

There is value in chairmen setting down some guiding principles when their companies reach such a size that they are no longer in regular personal contact with senior people throughout the enterprise. Such principles are particularly useful to those working in an international business. To compete in the markets of the world, managers on the spot have to be given as much operating freedom as possible. As companies extend geographically and as they devolve more responsibility from the centre to the operating units, there needs to be some means of holding the enterprise together in the face of these forces for fragmentation. I believe that the glue which holds a company together is its beliefs and values, rather than its structures and systems. We should be ready to learn from Japan and to accord the characters of our companies the importance they deserve.

CHAPTER 11

THE GOVERNANCE AGENDA

The governance of business, in other words, is likely to become an issue
throughout the developed world.

Peter Drucker

IDENTIFYING THE ISSUES

This final chapter considers some of the issues which seem likely to
engage the attention of chairmen over the next few years. It is not
easy to pick out those forces for change which will prove decisive in
the longer term. In the late 1970s, the central issue for the boards of
British companies appeared to be whether their unitary board
structure was going to be altered radically in the name of industrial
democracy. In the event, that particular approach to employee
involvement came to nothing and an issue which dominated board
thinking in Britain at the time is no longer on the agenda.

Peter Drucker, with his customary perception, identified corporate
governance as an issue for the future, when writing in *The Economist*
in 1989. The widespread nature of the governance debate since then
has decisively confirmed his conclusion and it is on governance-
related matters that I intend to focus. There are other agents of change
which are more all-pervasive, since they help to determine the
competitive environment within which companies carry on their
business.

They include advances in technology, the emergence of the newly
industrialised countries, the dismantling of state controls and the
increasing internationalisation of markets. Combined, they will make
competition more global and more intense. They will also have their
effect on governance: as companies and markets become more
international, those investing in them will look for common standards
of corporate direction and control. Their primary influence will, for

183

all that, be on the market-place and on the relationship between companies and their customers.

Corporate governance

Although the governance debate is relevant to companies in general, it centres in the first instance on those which are publicly quoted. For such companies, pressures to act on matters of governance will come from two main constituencies: first, shareholders, whose influence has grown markedly and will continue to grow. Shareholders are directly interested in how well the companies in which they have invested are run and also in their accountability – the one reinforces the other.

The second constituency is broader and embraces all those with an interest in governance standards. This grouping includes politicians, regulatory agencies, the professions and society more generally. The contribution of this constituency to the debate relates to such issues as the balance between self- and statutory regulation and how far governance structures and standards should be harmonised internationally.

The two constituencies interact and cannot be neatly divided. Their approach to governance matters is, however, different and so it is logical to treat them separately. The purpose of discussing the extent of their influence and their ability to bring about change is to identify which issues, under the broad heading of corporate governance, chairmen should have on their agendas and what impact they might have on the structure of their boards.

SHAREHOLDER INFLUENCE

Institutional investors

The change in the pattern of shareholding over the last thirty years and the rise of the institutional investor, particularly in Britain and the United States, have been well documented. The fact that the institutions now own such a high proportion of the shares of British public companies has given them both greater influence in company affairs and greater cause to use that influence. Collectively, they have a compelling incentive to improve the governance of the companies in which they have invested, rather than avoiding the issue by selling out – given that, broadly, they can only sell to each other.

Arguments for involvement

There are other reasons why the institutions are now taking a more direct interest in the governance of companies. In the United States, those who hold shares as trustees are required by law to use their votes and to be answerable for so doing. The obligation to vote extends to shares wherever they are held. Voting by American investors in Britain will reinforce the move, already well under way, for British institutions to use their votes actively at general meetings.

If investing institutions are to vote on governance issues, they need to understand the implications of those issues and determine their policy on them. This leads to a demand for analyses of resolutions coming up at shareholder meetings, which is being met by bodies like the National Association of Pension Funds and Pensions Investment Research Consultants, who issue *Shareholder Voting Guidelines*. The publication of their advice, in turn, creates interest in governance issues and encourages investors to cast their votes.

A financial argument for institutional involvement in matters of governance has been advanced by CalPERS, an $80 billion US pension fund. CalPERS commissioned an independent study to determine whether their policy of shareholder activism added value to their fund. The study concluded that the effort and resources that CalPERS put into improving the management of the companies in which they had invested, added $137m a year over a three-year period to the value of their portfolio. If Voice (using investor influence) pays, it becomes harder to justify Exit (selling out).

In addition to commercial arguments for investing institutions to become more positively involved in governance matters, there is now a general public expectation that they will. The institutions are seen as having the power to bring about change in the corporate system and a measure of duty to use it. The institutions, on their part, are now willing to shoulder responsibilities, individually and collectively, which they would not formerly have regarded as falling to them.

Board and shareholder responsibilities

This change of climate was reflected in a speech by the Governor of the Bank of England on 'The developing role and responsibilities of institutional shareholders', which was reported in the *Bank of England Quarterly Bulletin* for June 1986. In it, he said that the primary responsibility for the efficient running of companies lay with the companies themselves and that the most usual cause for their drifting into difficulties was 'when the board is not up to the job'. He then outlined the responsibilities which boards have towards their companies and added the following:

> Boards of directors do not have responsibilities of the kind that I have just described in, so to speak, a vacuum. They are accountable for discharging them, and this accountability is principally and very squarely in our system to the shareholders. The reciprocal of this obligation is the obligation of the shareholders to satisfy themselves about the competence of their boards and the way in which they are functioning.

This statement makes clear where the responsibilities of shareholders lie: not in the management of companies, but in ensuring that they are efficiently managed. Shareholders should monitor the competence of boards and press for action if they are not, in the Governor's words, 'up to the job'. Such action is increasingly seen as in their own interests and as part of their contribution to a more productive economy.

The Institutional Shareholders' Committee has set out the institutional stall in *The Responsibilities of Institutional Shareholders in the UK*, to which reference has already been made. In it, the Committee encourages its members to use their votes and to work more closely with companies in order to 'enable shareholders to gain a better appreciation of management's objectives, the problems confronting it and the quality of those involved, while also focusing the attention of management more sharply on the expectations and requirements of shareholders'. These are, therefore, matters which will figure on the agendas of chairmen.

Individual shareholders

While power lies with the institutions in terms of their votes, individual shareholders have played an influential part in the move to improve the effectiveness and accountability of boards. Shareholder associations are gaining strength and authority worldwide. The role of shareholders in governance has been well summarised in an authoritative and important book, *Power and Accountability*, by Robert A.G. Monks who is himself an active American investor. He writes as follows:

> Shareholders, as a matter of law and policy, must keep to a very limited set of issues. They do not have the expertise, the resources, or the right to become involved in matters of day-to-day management. Their

liability is limited to the amount of their investment. Their only involvement should be to make sure that the interests of directors and management are aligned with those of the shareholders, and that when a conflict of interest is presented, the shareholders make the decisions themselves.

Potential conflicts of interest can arise over such matters as directors' benefits, bids and buy-outs, top-level succession and the balance between the payment of dividends and reinvestment in the business. While the issues on which shareholders wish to have the power of decision may be limited, they are weighty. How, and how far, shareholder power should be exercised over them will find its place on the chairman's agenda.

Interest groups

Interest groups are a third force in the shareholder camp. They differ from institutions and individual shareholders in that they seek to influence some particular aspect of a company's activities. The pressures exerted by interest groups on boards can be expected to continue much as they have done in the past, but their focus will shift in line with what the community sees as its new priorities.

Environmental interests

Solicitude for the environment has moved towards the top of the social agenda and is being articulated in the United States by a body called the Social Investment Forum, which brings together investors concerned over social and ethical issues. The Forum began by asking all large American companies to sign a set of 'Valdez Principles', named after the 1989 environmental disaster. One of the ten Valdez Principles was: 'At least one member of the Board of Directors will be a person qualified to represent environmental interests.'

CERES Principles

This raised the whole question of the representation of interests, quite apart from how an environmental qualification should be defined. The Valdez Principles were rewritten as the CERES Principles in 1992, CERES standing for the Coalition for Environmentally Responsible Economies. The principle relating to board membership now reads: 'In selecting our Board of Directors, we will consider demonstrated environmental commitment as a factor.'

The significance of codes of this kind lies not so much in their aim of influencing the make-up of boards, as in the change to the terms of the contract between business and society which they represent. Companies work within boundaries set, formally and informally, by society. Environmental groups seek to alter these boundary lines, and companies have to enter the debate over how they should be redrawn, in order to ensure that the new boundaries pay due regard to the other interests involved. Boards need to take account of all relevant interests, of which the claims of the environment are one – albeit an increasingly insistent one. Boards also have to come to decisions leading to action, a responsibility which the promoters of principles are largely spared.

Summary

Shareholders, individually and collectively, are taking a more informed interest in the ways in which companies are directed and controlled. They are using their influence and their votes to increase the accountability of boards to investors. The tide of shareholder involvement has acquired a worldwide momentum of its own.

Although poor company results and some spectacular frauds and failures may have fanned the interest of shareholders in governance, it is now too firmly established to lapse when boom times return. Responsibilities once grasped are unlikely to be let slip, and the apparent success of shareholder groups in bringing about change on company boards, especially in the United States, will encourage shareholder activism. What are the practical consequences for chairmen and boards of this shift in the balance of power within the structure of corporate governance?

EXERCISE OF SHAREHOLDER INFLUENCE

Effect on corporate structure

One of the reactions of shareholders to their dissatisfaction with the track record of companies in which they had invested was to bring about changes in the way in which they were controlled. In the United States, small institutional and entrepreneurial groups took over control from more broadly based bodies of shareholders on quite a scale.

In an article in the September/October 1989 issue of the *Harvard Business Review*, Professor Michael Jensen chronicled the speed and magnitude of this transformation under the heading 'Eclipse of the public corporation'. Professor Jensen still saw a future for the accepted company structure in some sectors of the economy, but he argued against the continuation of shareholders and boards of the traditional kind in industries which did not have growth on their side. Included in the article is a note on the privatisation of equity by Professor Jay Light, which opens as follows:

> The last share of publicly traded common stock owned by an individual will be sold in the year 2003, if current trends persist. This forecast may be fanciful (short-term trends never persist) but the basic direction is clear. By the turn of the century, the primacy of public stock ownership in the United States may have all but disappeared.

Professor Light's forecast is, of course, fanciful and not just for the reason he gives. The public corporation has shown a remarkable ability to adapt and to survive, while the US pattern of privatisation of equity has not been repeated elsewhere.

Takeover bids

A more general assertion of shareholder power came with the rise of the takeover bid, an approach to changing the control of companies centred on those countries where shares were widely traded.

The logic behind the takeover approach was beguilingly simple and rested on two propositions. The first was that there should be as free a market as possible in the control of assets. The highest bidders for a business would, by definition, have perceived how best to earn the highest return from it and would have every incentive to prove themselves right. Thus standards of board effectiveness would be raised.

The second proposition was that the takeover process should largely be financed by debt. This would secure the accountability of directors to shareholders and prevent boards enlarging their empires, instead of returning cash to the shareholders in dividends. Successful bidders would have to concentrate on cash-flow to service their debt and would be subject to the disciplines of the market in raising new capital for expansion.

The theory was impeccable and appeared to address the twin criticisms of boards, that they were too often ineffective and that they were insufficiently accountable. The takeover process, it was argued, would raise board standards not only directly, in companies where control changed hands, but indirectly, in every company which saw itself as a potential target.

The track record of takeovers, however, has in general been unimpressive, quite apart from the fact that there are ways of changing the management of a company without going through the upheaval of taking it over. There are a number of reasons why the theoretical benefits of takeovers failed to live up to the claims of their promoters, among them the facts that their financial logic often proved stronger than their commercial logic, and that those who thought they could earn a better return from the assets which they acquired, turned out to be wrong.

Governance consequences

The takeover era had a number of governance consequences. First, it focused the attention of boards on returns in the short term. Acquirers had to concentrate on generating immediate cash to service and pay off debt, while potential target companies had to watch their share price daily.

Second, it cast shareholders and boards in opposition to one another and assumed that the best results were achieved under threat. The implied message from shareholders to boards was – either perform or we put the business up for sale. Faced with this adversarial relationship, directors dug in and protected their positions with a range of legal, financial and political defences. This had the unintended, but foreseeable, result of making it more difficult to bring about boardroom change, which had been the basic objective of the takeover process.

This concentration on short-term results and the defensive position taken up by boards led to a reappraisal by shareholders of the best ways of furthering their aims. The emphasis switched from encouraging bids for companies, to bringing about change from within. If investors could use their power to persuade boards to ensure that their companies were managed more in line with the interests of their shareholders, the risks and adverse consequences of takeovers could largely be avoided.

The shareholder agenda

The present shareholder agenda, therefore, is likely to centre on ways of increasing the influence of investors in the manner in which companies are directed and controlled. That influence can be exercised directly through voting and indirectly by persuasion; it can also be exercised individually or collectively. What are the main issues which shareholders are likely to wish to address and how will they go about addressing them?

One issue will be the composition and structure of company boards. This covers the balance between executive and outside directors, the division of responsibilities at the head of a company and the establishment of appropriate board committees. I would expect particular attention to be paid to the process through which directors are chosen and to the contribution which they are individually expected to make.

Another issue, which follows on naturally, will be the strategies and policies set by the board. Under this heading would come the company's plans for development and their financing, dividend policy and the way in which the company discharges its external responsibilities.

A third set of issues will revolve around potential conflicts between the interests of shareholders and managers. This has surfaced most recently and publicly over directors' terms and conditions.

Shareholder action

I would expect shareholders to pursue these matters both individually and through their associations. Institutional investors have the advantage of being able to put their points direct to company boards, and a leading British pension fund management company has recently used its influence to reduce the length of directors' contracts. Equally, the institutions acting together have published guidelines on share option schemes and on executive remuneration.

For individual shareholders, the focus is likely to be on restoring a sense of purpose to general meetings, with a special emphasis on the election of directors and on boards accounting for their stewardship. This cause is attracting support from the institutions as well, with one of them calling recently for 'the resuscitation of the AGM'.

Shareholder committees

A more open question is whether shareholder committees will come to play the same role in Britain as they have in the United States, where they have had their own candidates appointed to boards. The problem with shareholder committees is that their legitimacy depends on how representative they are of the general body of shareholders. An American way of short-circuiting the problem is to draw the committee only from major investors who have held their shares for a certain length of time. These limitations make the process of forming a committee manageable, at the expense of it being representative; shareholder committees are not on the agenda of the UK Shareholders' Association at present.

The need for dialogue

What many of these points add up to is the need for closer links between shareholders and boards. This point was addressed by Sir Brian Corby, when he was chief executive of the Prudential Corporation, speaking at an International Stock Exchange Conference in 1989:

> First we have to improve the two-way dialogue between companies and shareholders. It requires continuous, not spasmodic, effort to do this. The relationship has to be a more robust one with management prepared to offer information and shareholders prepared to put forward views. Above all, both must be prepared to listen. Dialogue is not always going to be easy but it must be capable of being conducted without acrimony. This should be particularly possible if the process is a continuous one.

The Code of Best Practice of the Committee on the Financial Aspects of Corporate Governance should assist the dialogue by providing a framework within which it can usefully take place. The test from the shareholders' point of view will be the degree to which the dialogue leads to action.

THE EXTERNAL INFLUENCES ON BOARDS

The regulatory approach

The debate over the future direction of corporate governance is not simply between boards and shareholders. Politicians, regulatory authorities, professional institutions, commentators and the public have views on where the problems lie and how they should be resolved. Governments are responsible for the legal structure of governance. The regulatory authorities determine the obligations which companies must meet, if they are to raise money from the public. Accountants and lawyers have professional responsibilities towards companies, while commentators and the public make their own judgements about where the line between acceptable and unacceptable corporate conduct should be drawn.

The link between these diverse groups is that they have an interest in raising governance standards. What separates them, or their constituents, is the degree to which they believe that this can be brought about statutorily. The familiar arguments for statutory regulation are that anything less will be ignored by those most in need of it and that this will put those who already meet accepted standards at a competitive disadvantage.

Statutory regulation

The arguments against statutory regulation are equally familiar. It is costly, inefficient, slow to react and simply sets a floor. My doubts about statutory intervention, in this particular field, concern whether it will work. For example, what matters is the quality of board members, not their number, nor the division between executive and outside directors, all of which are the stuff of regulation. Similarly, regulation can determine that publicly quoted companies split the posts of chairman and of chief executive, but not that responsibilities are appropriately divided between them. The further disadvantage of regulations is that compliance with their letter weakens the shareholders' grounds for challenge when their intent is not being met.

Market regulation

The Committee on the Financial Aspects of Corporate Governance has relied on what could best be described as market regulation to bring about compliance with its Code of Best Practice. In other words, abiding by the Code will improve the market standing of companies and therefore will be in their self-interest and that of their shareholders. At the same time, the Committee left the way in which the Code was implemented and the degree to which companies conformed to it, as a matter between boards and their shareholders. The market, rather than the law or the sense of duty of directors, would thus become the arbiter of governance standards.

Market regulation puts the responsibility on chairmen and boards to be aware of what their shareholders and society expect of them and to act accordingly. Failure to do so will be reflected in the share price. This approach will not, however, necessarily carry the day with politicians.

The politics of governance

Winning for Britain – Labour's Strategy for Success states that the Labour Party will monitor progress on the reforms proposed by the

Committee on the Financial Aspects of Corporate Governance, in order to establish whether it would be desirable to provide a minimum legal standard for the composition of boards. It goes on to comment on board structure and board composition in these terms:

> We believe that a supervisory board could provide a valuable forum for focus on longer-term strategy of the company and we will provide a statutory basis for a two-tier board structure for those larger companies who choose to adopt it.
>
> If industrial corporations are to gain security through the broadest collective support, it is essential that non-executive directors are not regarded as representing solely the interests of shareholders. We share the analysis of the RSA Report on Tomorrow's Company that the successful company of the future will be one that emphasises long-term co-operative relationships and fosters structures that include key stakeholders such as suppliers, employees and the community in corporate development.
>
> We believe that in the appointment of non-executive directors companies should recognise that there are other stakeholders in the future of the company than shareholders.

These passages raise a number of points for chairmen to ponder. In the first place, the two-tier board is put forward simply as an option. It is not clear what statutory basis for it the authors of the document have in mind. The Companies Acts concentrate on the responsibilities of directors and until the 1989 Act they made no reference to boards nor to their structure. There is still no definition of a board of directors in the Companies Acts. Thus it would seem that companies can adopt whatever board pattern they and their shareholders think fit, by re-writing their articles of association to that effect.

A British unitary board could, by that means, divide itself into what might be termed a governing board and a management board, with the approval of its shareholders. This would clarify the responsibilities of the directors sitting on the two boards and separate the functions of framing policy and of executing it. Such a structure would not, however, be recognised in the European Union as a two-tier board. Supervisory boards and management boards, in the Union two-tier structure, are separate organs of the company and have different legal responsibilities. A divided unitary board would remain, in law, a single organ of the company and the directors of its two components would have equal legal responsibilities.

A further point is that the establishment of a statutory basis for a two-tier board would logically entail establishing a statutory basis for a unitary board. This would assist in defining the responsibilities of directors, but would be a more formidable undertaking than the authors of *Labour's Strategy for Success* probably had in mind.

Tomorrow's Company

Second, there is the reference to the Royal Society of Arts' Report on *Tomorrow's Company*. The RSA enquiry looks ahead to the future shape of boards. It is business-driven and is tackling such fundamental questions as the purpose of companies and how the pursuit of their purpose can be objectively measured. It is important that the governance debate should not be limited to existing board systems and the RSA enquiry provides a framework within which the debate can be continued constructively to arrive at practical conclusions.

An issue which is addressed in the RSA enquiry and referred to in the Labour Party document is how far boards should be accountable to groups other than their shareholders. Chairmen and boards recognise the degree to which their companies depend on the support of all the links in their particular business chain, but there are real problems about widening the responsibilities of directors beyond their duty to their company. There is the danger of confusion and that of diffused accountability becoming diminished accountability.

THE EUROPEAN DIMENSION

The discussion of external sources of influence on governance now needs to be broadened to take in British membership of the European Union. Companies are already working within a single European market and either political or market forces could bring about changes in governance systems across the Union. The political force would stem from efforts by the European Commission to bring about some degree of harmonisation of board structures throughout the Union. Market forces might equally bring about convergence, if one form of governance structure seemed to offer a competitive advantage.

Harmonisation proposals

The European Commission has published proposals for a European Company Statute in the form of a draft Regulation, which deals with company law and taxation, and a draft Directive covering employee participation. The object of the Statute is to enable companies to be set up which can operate across the Union, governed by European rather than national regulations. The formation of European companies under this Statute is at present an option and one which is open to any enterprise wishing to take advantage of its provisions.

Even though companies already doing business in Europe may not be intending to set up European companies of this kind, they will find the Statute worth studying as a pointer to the future. Its proposals are complex, because they include a number of options to cover the different board models that have evolved in the countries within the Union. The key proposals in the Statute relate to board structure and to employee involvement.

Board structure

On board structure, the Statute offers a choice between a two-tier or single-tier board. Under the two-tier option, there is a supervisory board which appoints and monitors the management board. At least one-third and not more than one-half of the members of the supervisory board have to be appointed by the employees. The supervisory board must receive quarterly reports on the progress of the business and can call for additional information on company matters at any time (this represents a strengthening of the existing rights of a supervisory board).

The single-tier option consists of an administrative board, on which non-executive members must be in the majority. All members of the administrative board are now to have the same rights and obligations – a concession to Britain – but the Statute still lays down that the main function of the non-executive members is to supervise the executive members. Its form is, therefore, that of a unitary board, but the executive and non-executive directors do not have precisely the same functions. Employees may be represented on the administrative board along the lines of their representation on the supervisory board in the two-tier option; they may also be represented through separate bodies by collective agreement. The Statute prescribes minimum requirements for informing and consulting employees.

There are likely to be tax incentives to encourage businesses to form European companies and, in time, their structure could become mandatory rather than optional. The thinking behind the European Company Statute is, therefore, of practical relevance to most companies within the Union. It also indicates the direction which the drive to reform and to harmonise the structure of European enterprises is likely to take.

Employee involvement

The emphasis which the European Company Statute puts on employee involvement at board level raises an issue for the future, which seems never to be discussed. This is that employee representation on boards is feasible for a national company, but impractical for an international enterprise.

The descriptions of co-determination in Germany, for example, refer to half the members of the supervisory boards of companies, employing more than 2,000 people, being representatives of the employees. A more accurate statement would be that half the seats on the upper boards of these companies are filled by representatives of the German employees. So long as the main centres of employment of these companies were in their home territory, this system met the aim of ensuring that the views of employees were taken into account at the highest level of governance, and the distinction between nationals and others was unimportant. Now that so many of these companies have operations outside Germany, confining employee representation on the supervisory board to Germans becomes increasingly anomalous.

In addition, it has two consequences for the boards concerned. One is to build something of a mercantilist bias into the board structure. The employee members of the supervisory board of a German company considering transferring production overseas might understandably oppose the project. They are there to represent the interests of those who elected them, not the interests of all employees, including those abroad who might benefit from the transfer.

Another consequence is that it brings about an imbalance on the supervisory board. The employee members represent a national interest, while the other members have to have regard to the company's international interests.

The question of how employees should be involved in the enterprises in which they work is of concern to chairmen and boards, inside and outside the European Union. The parochial nature of the German co-determination model looks increasingly out of place in a world where companies operate and compete globally. The logical way forward in Europe is to pay more attention to methods of involving employees, other than through board representation. The aim of involvement is to give employees an effective say in the decisions which touch them most directly, before those decisions are taken. The majority of such decisions never reach the board. This suggests that involvement is more relevant at the workplace than at the board and is better built from the bottom up than from the top down.

Basic governance differences

As a footnote to the European board scene, it is important to appreciate that there is a fundamental difference between the Anglo/ American and the Continental European concept of the nature of a company. In America and Britain, companies are seen as enterprises based on the capital invested in them by the shareholders. The key relationship in a capitalistic enterprise is between owners and managers; hence the emphasis in Britain on the rights and responsibilities of shareholders.

The Continental view is much more along the lines of companies being partnerships between capital and labour. They are seen as coalitions of interests and as serving a wider purpose than providing a return to shareholders. Emphasis is, therefore, placed on the relationship with employees in the Continental model and on the place of the company in the community. This is in contrast to the rights of shareholders, especially minority shareholders, which have traditionally received scant consideration.

There is a second difference which is relevant in the governance context. In America and Britain, self-regulation is generally preferred to statutory control. This is because self-regulation puts the responsibility where it belongs, at the point where decisions are made, and because it focuses on keeping to the spirit rather than to the letter of the law. The concept of corporate self-regulation is alien to the Continental European tradition.

The state of play

There seems, at present, to be no great enthusiasm within the European Commission for harmonising corporate governance, although the harmonisation of company law remains an aim. The Fifth Company Law Directive covers such matters as the duties of directors, the rights of minority shareholders, the conduct of general meetings and the structure of boards. It has not yet been adopted by the Council and its provisions for employee involvement have proved a stumbling-block. Germany fears legislation which might be used to water down its present system of co-determination, while Britain wishes to retain its non-legislative approach to joint consultation and collective bargaining. There is a similar divide over the European

Company Statute, which as a result has not yet been agreed by the Council.

Quite apart from differences of view over the place of the law in matters of governance, corporate structures and systems vary so widely within the present European Union – let alone an enlarged one – that harmonisation could only be brought about over an extended period. I would expect a degree of convergence over time, with British companies giving greater formal recognition to their responsibilities towards employees and with Continental European companies having to meet Anglo/American standards of disclosure and financial reporting. Chairmen will need to keep a watching brief on governance developments within the Union, but I would not expect them to be high on their agenda.

THE CHAIRMAN'S AGENDA

The Code of Best Practice

An issue which will be on the agenda of chairmen of listed companies registered in the United Kingdom is the Code of Best Practice, to which reference has already been made. Three principles run through the Code and it is for chairmen and boards to determine how they should be applied in the particular circumstances of their own companies. The first principle is that of *disclosure*. Disclosure ensures that all those with a legitimate interest in a company have the information which they require in order to exercise their rights and responsibilities towards it. In addition, openness by companies is the basis of public confidence in the corporate system.

The second principle is that there should be *appropriate checks and balances* within the governance structure, particularly at board level. This is to assist the directors in fulfilling their duty to act always in the interests of the company and to guard against undue concentrations of power. The third principle is that there should be *absolute clarity* about where the responsibilities for financial control and reporting lie.

Chairmen have a direct interest in the application of all these principles within their companies. They answer for them through the statement of compliance with the Code in the Annual Report and increasingly through a governance statement as well. One such statement from a major company is entitled 'How we run the company'; this is just what investors and employees want to know and such statements will encourage constructive dialogues between shareholders and boards.

An issue which will certainly be on the agenda of chairmen is the composition of their boards. This arises partly from the Code and also from the interest which institutional investors are taking in this aspect of governance. Equally, there is growing interest in whether and how boards assess their performance. These last two points, in particular, and other governance matters are picked up in the guidelines recently adopted by General Motors of the United States.

GM's guidelines

GM's new guidelines on the role of its board of directors provide a practical example of how a major American company is addressing a number of items on the governance agenda. In effect, the GM board has drawn up its own Code of Best Practice. It includes the appointment by the outside directors of a lead director from among their number, the establishment of board committees, the provision of board information, the selection of board candidates, the assessment of board performance and the formal evaluation of the CEO. It is worth quoting the guidelines on board composition and performance assessment, given the references already made to these two matters:

> the Committee on Director Affairs is responsible for reviewing with the Board on an annual basis the appropriate skills and characteristics required of board members in the context of the current make-up of the Board. This assessment should include issues of diversity, age, skills such as understanding of manufacturing technologies, international background, etc. – all in the context of an assessment of the perceived needs of the Board at that point in time. The Board itself should be responsible, in fact as well as procedure, for selecting its own members.

In respect of board performance the guideline runs as follows:

> The Committee on Director Affairs is responsible to report annually to the Board an assessment of the Board's performance. This will be discussed with the full Board. This should be done following the end of each fiscal year and at the same time as the report on board membership criteria. The assessment should be of the Board's contribution as a whole and specifically review areas in which the Board and/or the Management believes a better contribution could be made.

The guidelines institutionalise structures and processes which were previously left to the board of the time to decide. They add rigour to the way in which the board works and provide benchmarks against which the performance of the chairman, the CEO and the board can be measured. In addition to its own code, GM has signed up on the CERES Principles.

The main reason for including these references to GM is to illustrate some of the current governance issues facing chairmen and how one board is dealing with them. At the same time, it exemplifies a shift in the balance of power within the governance structure. The GM board has strengthened its grip on the business and the outside directors have taken the lead in identifying the need for change and in setting its direction. It is not a matter of the board increasing its power at the expense of the shareholders, but doing so internally in relation to management. Indeed, in setting the guidelines in place, the outside chairman of the GM board stressed that the aim was to strengthen the board's accountability to shareholders.

Shareholder relations

That affirmation leads naturally on to the relationship between boards and shareholders. I would expect there to be three main items under this heading on the chairman's agenda – board nominations, board accountability and communications with shareholders, all of which have already been tabled.

Board nominations

First, shareholders are looking for a greater say in the selection and appointment of board members, to bring the theoretical model of corporate governance nearer to reality. The establishment of properly constituted nomination committees of the board is a first step and a second would be to make it easier for shareholders to put forward their own candidates and to reject those whom they felt were insufficiently qualified. Provided shareholder nominations lengthened the list of qualified, independent board candidates, this would strengthen the authority of the board and accord more weight to the views of shareholders.

Board accountability

Next, the main opportunity for shareholders to hold boards accountable for their stewardship is at the AGM. The issue here, therefore, is finding ways of making the AGM a more useful governance occasion for both boards and shareholders. This would include removing some of the barriers to shareholders putting

forward resolutions at general meetings and informing the shareholder body as a whole of the outcome of AGM discussions, as Grand
Metropolitan have done.

Communications

Last on the list is the more general question of improving
communications between boards and shareholders, again to their joint
advantage. The need for dialogue has already been discussed and it is
helpful that one of the principles of good practice proposed by the
Institutional Shareholders' Committee is the following:

> Institutional investors should encourage regular, systematic contact at
> senior executive level to exchange views and information on strategy,
> performance, Board membership and quality of management.

I am hesitant about the inclusion of 'performance' on that agenda,
since it could be interpreted in a current and immediate sense. The
other headings look ahead to longer-term factors which will
determine a company's progress and development and on which
dialogue can most usefully be centred. What has to come out of the
dialogue is a thorough understanding by shareholders of their board's
future aims and a degree of confidence in their ability to achieve them.
It will primarily be up to chairmen and their boards to work at this
relationship, but it will require an equivalent response from the
institutions.

Institutional accountability

There is a final aspect of the relationship between shareholders and
boards, which will appear on the agenda of chairmen of investing
institutions, although it has not yet entered the governance debate.
Institutions are rightly casting their votes as shareholders and will
increasingly do so. Through the voting process, boards of the
companies in which the institutions have invested are being held more
closely to account by their shareholders. That, however, puts an onus
on the institutions to show that they are equally accountable to those
who have invested in them, and on whose behalf they are voting. The
chain of accountability extends beyond boards to institutional
shareholders, and on to those for whose benefit the institutions hold
their shares.

Conclusions on board structure

Two-tier boards?

Having discussed what is on the agenda for chairmen, this is an appropriate point at which to move an issue towards the bottom of the agenda, if not off it altogether. I would not expect there to be pressure from shareholders, politicians or the European Commission for British companies to abandon unitary boards in favour of the two-tier model. It could be argued that the two-tier system is inherently more robust from the shareholders' point of view than its unitary equivalent – it was after all introduced in Germany to strengthen the hand of shareholders. If there is doubt about the calibre of the members of a board, a two-tier structure possibly provides more protection against disaster than a unitary one.

Given, however, the more active part which shareholders are beginning to play in corporate governance, they are likely to stay with systems with whose workings they are familiar. In countries where choice of board structure has been introduced, few companies have availed themselves of it. The logic of sticking to your last, in matters of governance, is that the structural design of boards is not ultimately decisive. Structure is important; its precise form is less so. The effectiveness of governance systems depends primarily on the clarity with which responsibilities are assigned within them and the quality of the people who undertake those responsibilities.

As Demb and Neubauer's researches show, the way in which boards in practice are involved in matters of governance vary remarkably, even within the same national setting. What matters is that the principles of sound governance should be observed, within whatever structure boards and their shareholders choose to adopt.

Challenges to the unitary principle

Having said that, a marker needs to be put down in respect of two features of the unitary board system. The first concerns the legal basis of the board's unity. This is founded on the concept of all directors having broadly equal responsibilities and duties. If a significant legal distinction were to be drawn between the responsibilities of executive and outside directors, then a two-tier structure would have been created within a unitary board. This would lead in logic to a formal move to the two-tier system.

AWA v. Daniels

In a landmark judgment delivered in Australia in July 1992, in the case of *AWA Limited* v. *Daniels*, the judge made the following observation:

> One of the most striking features of the law concerning directors' duties is the insistence that directors accept more and more responsibility for oversight of a company's affairs at the same time as the affairs of companies become more and more complex and diverse. What knowledge of the affairs of an international conglomerate like IBM or General Motors can a non-executive director be required or expected to have? As conglomerates get larger and more complex it becomes almost impossible for the non-executive director to discharge directorial duties in any detailed and knowledgeable manner.

Following that reasoning, the judge found that the senior management of AWA were negligent, including its chairman who was also the chief executive, but he exonerated the non-executive directors. Whatever the final outcome of the case, there is a refreshing whiff of realism about the judge's conclusions on corporate governance. If the judgment stands and is built on, then the unitary board will be under legal pressure to divide in two.

Divided views

The second potential challenge to the unitary board approach comes from within; it is reflected in differences of view among board members as to what they are there for. Recent surveys on how directors see their responsibilities have drawn attention to the gap between executive and outside directors in their perception of their roles.

For example, a survey by Egon Zehnder International concluded: 'Chief executives and their non-executive directors disagree as to the optimal level of involvement by non-executive directors. Non-executives want much more influence than chief executives want them to have, and non-executives desire a much more active role in developing and monitoring strategy than chief executives want to see.'

In the same vein, a research study sponsored by PRO NED and the London Stock Exchange in 1992 found that two-thirds of the outside directors taking part believed that they could usefully be involved in the development of strategy, and that they should be – a view shared by fewer than one-third of the chief executives in the same sample.

The indication from these surveys is that a majority of executive directors would prefer outside directors to concentrate on supervision and to leave issues like strategy to them. Outside directors, on the other hand, feel that they are not being encouraged or allowed to make the contribution to the development of the business of which they are capable. If the executive view expressed in these surveys were to prevail, executive directors would be transferring their responsibilities for supervision to the outside directors, while diminishing the role of the outside directors in the rest of the board's activities. Such a move would, in effect, establish a two-tier division of duties.

Board unity

I said in the Introduction that I would return to the criticism that the recommendations of the Committee on the Financial Aspects of Corporate Governance would undermine the unitary nature of the board. The Committee's proposals do not of themselves alter the responsibilities of either outside or executive directors. The Committee was dealing solely with the financial aspects of corporate governance and therefore underlined the role of the outside directors on board committees and over issues where independence of judgement was required. The Report, however, emphasised that all directors shared the responsibility for supervision and said, 'It is equally for chairmen to ensure that executive directors look beyond their executive duties and accept their full share of the responsibilities of governance.'

All members of a unitary board are equally responsible in law for their board's actions and decisions. That said, executive and outside directors have different contributions to make to the board's work. They are involved in the company to different degrees and they bring different perspectives to bear on board issues. Their ability to work together as a board team is dependent on the care with which they have been selected and more particularly on their chairman.

ACTION BY CHAIRMEN

The items already discussed in relation to shareholders, Europe and the Code of Best Practice are all likely to find their place on the agenda of chairmen. The central issue for chairmen, however, may be not so much the nature of the items on the agenda, as the effectiveness of their boards in dealing with them. The AWA judgment is a reminder of just how complex a task a board has in directing and controlling a business. Directing an enterprise through a board is a more difficult form of governance than is commonly supposed. It is a fundamental error to regard committees of any kind as natural forms of governance, or to believe that if you sit competent people of goodwill round a boardroom table, they will function as a board.

All this is particularly true of a unitary board. Its potential advantages are its singleness of purpose and its capacity to integrate inside knowledge and outside experience in the service of the company. Turning that potential into reality is the job of the chairman. The advantages which the unitary form has to offer are unlikely to be realised if executive and outside directors disagree about their respective roles. A starting-point for chairmen is, therefore, to win agreement on the purpose of their boards and then agreement on how executive and outside directors can best work together in pursuit of that purpose.

Members of an effective board work together as a team, but retain their independence of judgement; they also balance their loyalties to each other and to the company. These are just some of the tensions at work within a board, and without the right degree of tension boards would be too comfortable and complacent to do their job. It is for chairmen to manage these tensions constructively. As Clutterbuck and Waine point out in *The Independent Board Director*:

> Getting the balance of creative, positive conflict right is one of the chairman's most difficult tasks.

There has to be a balance on a board between individuality and collegiality and between continuity and change. It is chairmen who are responsible for finding these crucial points of balance.

I am convinced that we underestimate the difficulty of getting the best out of a unitary board. It depends far more than is generally realised on the competence of the chairman. It is because the task of the chairman is so demanding that, all other reasons apart, I would not make it harder by combining the chairman's post with that of the chief executive.

The position of the chairman

It is only when the importance of the chairman's role is more generally recognised, that sufficient attention will be paid to what the chairman's job entails. Chairmanship has to be seen for what it is, a professional task, and not as an honorific distinction. Chairmen need to learn their craft through experience and through studying how others chair meetings. They have to understand the structure of the body which they are chairing, where the levers of power within it lie and what the key factors are that determine its success or failure.

Chairmen should, therefore, be familiar with the memorandum and articles of association of their companies and with *Robert's Rules of Order*, or some equivalent guide to committee procedures. Chairmen need to know the rules governing meetings not just in order to apply them, but to be aware of the reasoning which lies behind them, based as it is on the experience of their predecessors through the centuries. It is also helpful if chairmen have some appreciation of the way in which groups behave, to guide them in bringing out the best in the members of their boards individually and collectively.

The passage from the Heidrick and Struggles report, quoted in the opening chapter, showed the degree of confusion felt by chairmen about the nature and the definition of their responsibilities. The first step towards resolving those confusions is for chairmen to be clear about their duties and to agree them with their boards. Equally, the more opportunities which chairmen can find to meet their fellow-chairmen and to debate the essence of their role, the better.

More chances for chairmen to learn from each other, better provision for training in chairmanship and a greater readiness to write about the subject would all have their place in raising the standards of those who take the chair and thereby the standing of chairmen. Effective boards demand effective chairmen.

REFLECTIONS ON CHAIRMANSHIP

Looking back on what I have written, I hope that this book will promote discussion about the responsibilities of chairmen and the ways in which these can best be carried out. Given the variety of chairmen and of companies, chairmen have to work out their own individual roles for themselves in conjunction with their boards.

I have not attempted to list the qualities which might be required of a chairman. This is partly because they have to be much the same as those needed for success in any other field of human endeavour and partly because I am not sure how useful job criteria of that kind are. It is undoubtedly helpful for a chairman to have a sense of humour, but senses of humour are matters of opinion and it is not clear what those who are told they do not possess one, should do about it. I have not, therefore, dealt in such classical virtues as integrity and judgement, which are perhaps more inherent than acquired. But there are other chairmanly attributes which are easier to define and to cultivate.

One is not to talk too much from the chair. As time goes by, it becomes more difficult to resist the temptation to reminisce, or to bring the discussion at the board on to familiar ground in order to be able to take full part in it. The chairman's job is to listen and not to chatter. Chairmen are there to orchestrate the discussion, so that it comes to a fruitful conclusion. The test is straightforward: how much of the board's discussion time is taken up by the chairman?

A second chairmanly attribute is the ability to integrate, to pull together the different threads of a complex issue, so that it acquires coherence. The skills of management are becoming increasingly specialised and so the fields of experience of directors are tending to become narrower. As a result, their approach to issues is likely to be determined by their particular expertise. The chairman, however, has to see the business as a whole, in the context of its environment, and needs to integrate the skills and perceptions of all those seated round the board table.

The principles to which I believe chairmen and their boards should work have come up regularly, but in different forms, throughout the book. Openness is one of them – the need to be open to ideas and open in explaining the company's actions and intentions. Openness is particularly important in dealing with people. Balance is another of them – the duty to weigh up the consequences of decisions on all those who will be affected by them and to hold the scales between the demands of today and the needs of tomorrow.

A third principle is the well-established one that rights and responsibilities go together. Chairmen, therefore, have responsibilities towards their boards, as do boards towards their chairmen. Companies have responsibilities towards society, but so does society to companies. Boards have their obligations to their shareholders and shareholders have them to their boards. Boards and their companies have to establish where they stand in an ever-changing network of duties owed and owing.

The chairman's place in all this does perhaps come nearest to that of the conductor of an orchestra; thus it is appropriate to close with Sir Ralph Vaughan Williams' words:

> All their art and all their skill are valueless without that corporate imagination which distinguishes the orchestra from a fortuitous collection of players.

It is for chairmen to capture that corporate imagination.

APPENDIX 1

Cadbury Schweppes earns it living in a competitive world. It needs to do so successfully to meet its obligations to all those with a stake in the enterprise and to make the Company one to which people are proud to belong.

We are in business to meet the needs of consumers internationally for products and services of good value and consistent quality. Our success in doing so is measured by the profitable growth of Cadbury Schweppes and by the advancement of its reputation.

The basis of our business is the goodwill of our customers, since we depend on literally millions of repeat purchases daily. The Company's main commercial assets are its brands and it is our responsibility to develop the markets for them. Cadbury Schweppes' brands are a guarantee to consumers of quality and value and we must invest consistently in building their reputation.

In setting out what the Company needs to become, I find no conflict between the values and characteristics we have inherited from the past and the actions we have to take to ensure a successful and independent future for Cadbury Schweppes. We cannot, however, depend on our history to carry us forward. The realities of the market-place are tough and demanding and the Company has to be able to respond rapidly to them. We need to build on the Company's undoubted strengths and to apply them in ways which are appropriate to overcoming the challenges ahead. The characteristics which I believe we must cultivate to succeed are:

Competitive ability

Cadbury Schweppes must be competitive in the market-place. To succeed, our products and services must maintain their identity and their edge against the competition. We compete on quality, value and service and so we must make the most of all the assets of the business. This means innovating and taking risks, while using research and analysis to increase the success rate, not to put decisions off. We are competing in the markets of the world, so we need to combine local initiative with dedication to the long-term interests of the Company as a whole. We are competing in today's markets and in tomorrow's, so profit now must be matched with consistent and imaginative investment in the future.

Clear objectives

Effective competition demands clarity of purpose. Objectives must be attainable, but require us to stretch our abilities, not work within them. Objectives need to be built from the bottom up, but set from the top down. When unit or individual objectives have been fixed, the debate is over and the focus is on their single-minded achievement. All objectives end with individuals, who are accountable for results and therefore must know precisely for what they are to be held accountable. But since the success of the Company depends on the sum of these individual efforts, what counts is the way they are co-ordinated. Everyone in the Company should understand what their individual and team objectives are and how they fit into the wider purpose of the business.

Taking advantage of change

Change is constant – in markets, in ideas, in people and in technology. In an uncertain and changing world we therefore need decisive leadership and trading units which are quick on their feet. We have to look ahead to the opportunities which change presents and to use the past only as a staging-post on the way forward. We must accept the risks which attend new ventures; above all we need people with enquiring minds, restlessly searching for new and better ways of advancing the Company. Meeting the challenge of change requires us to adapt to new patterns of work, new jobs and new careers and to seek the training which will make the best of these changes, in our own and the Company's interests. The aim is to encourage openness to new ideas and a readiness to adapt to changing needs.

Simple organisation

We must concentrate on the core tasks of the business and justify every support activity and every level of authority on the value which they add to the goods and services we sell. The basic building-blocks of the organisation are the business units, managed by integrated teams in direct touch with their markets. All decisions should be taken as near their point of impact as possible. This freedom of operating action carries with it the responsibility to use the strengths and resources of the Cadbury Schweppes Group where appropriate and to keep the aims of the units in line with those of the Company as a whole. The more straightforward the organisation and the way in which it arrives at decisions, the speedier its response, the more readily it can be adapted, the more satisfying it is to work in and the lower the cost it imposes on those it is there to serve. Building up informal links avoids organisational arthritis.

Committed people

The Company is made up of individuals and its success turns on their collective commitment to its aims. That commitment can only be won through our ability to bring about a convergence of individual, team and company goals. People should know what is expected of them and be given every help to meet those expectations. Our standards should be demanding, and demanding standards require appropriate rewards. Belief in the ability of people to grow means planning to promote from within, except when an outside infusion is needed. Equally, it means that where we fail with people, the situation must be faced up to openly and promptly and resolved with the least loss of individual self-respect, because the failure is shared. In the same way the responsibility for the development of people is shared, the drive must come from the individual and the training resources from the Company. Everyone in the Company should be encouraged to make the most of their abilities.

Openness

The principle of openness should apply in all our dealings inside and outside the Company. It follows that we should keep everyone in the business as well informed as possible within the legal limits of confidentiality. It also implies a readiness to listen. I believe in an open style of management and in involving people in the decisions which affect them, because it is right to do so and because it helps to bring individual and Company aims closer together. The responsibility for decisions rests on those appointed to take them, but if they are arrived at openly, the decisions are likely to be better and the commitment to them greater. Openness and trust are the basis of good working relationships on which the effectiveness of the organisation depends. They imply an acceptance of the mutual balance of rights and duties between individuals and the Company.

Responsibility

The Company recognises its obligations to all who have a stake in its success – shareholders, employees, customers, suppliers, governments and society – and seeks to keep its responsibilities to them in balance. We aim to act as good corporate citizens throughout the world and believe that international companies which follow that approach benefit their host countries. We believe in open competition and in doing business wherever there are suitable markets open to our trade. We seek to maintain the Company's reputation for meeting society's legitimate expectations of the business and for contributing to the life of the communities of which we are a part. We support worthwhile causes related to the Company's place in society and we encourage members of the Company to play their part in trade and public affairs.

Quality

The key characteristic we aim for in every aspect of the Company's activities is quality. Our products sell on their quality and their reputation is in the hands of each individual and unit throughout the Cadbury Schweppes business. An early Cadbury statement of aims reads:

> Our policy for the future as in the past will be: first, the best possible quality – nothing is too good for the public.

We must always be searching to improve quality and to add measurable value to the goods and services we market. But quality applies to people and to relationships, as well as to our working lives. We should set high standards and expect to be judged by them. The quality we aim for in all our dealings is that of integrity; the word 'integrity' means straight dealing but it also means completeness. Both meanings are relevant in this context, because the quality standard cannot be applied in part; it must be consistently applied to everything which bears the Company's name.

CONCLUSION

Cadbury Schweppes' concern for the values I have described will not be judged by this statement, but by our actions. The character of the Company is collectively in our hands. We have inherited its reputation and standing and it is for us to advance them. Pride in what we do is important to every one of us in the business and encourages us to give of our best; it is the hallmark of a successful company. Let us earn that pride by the way we put the beliefs set out here into action.

APPENDIX 2

GENESIS

Scepticism about the effectiveness of boards has an honourable history. August Detoeuf published this account of a board's activities in 'Propos de O.L. Barenton Confiseur' more than fifty years ago.

LA GENÈSE

Au commencement, il n'y avait que le Conseil.

Le premier jour, il créa l'assemblée générale, et se fit reconnaître par elle comme le Maître de toutes choses.

Le deuxième jour, il nomma le Président.

Le troisième jour, il nomma le Secrétaire.

Le quatrième jour, il répartit les tantièmes.

Le cinquième jour, il répartit les jetons de présence.

Le sixième jour, il choisit un homme et le nomma Directeur. Puis il lui dit: 'Tu travailleras à la sueur de ton front.'

Le septième jour, le huitième jour, et les jours suivants, jusqu'au jour béni de la Saint-Glinglin, le Conseil, ayant tout fait, se reposa.

Et il eut raison: car le Directeur se trouva bon.

This can be translated into less elegant English as follows:

GENESIS

In the beginning there was a Board of Directors.

On the first day it created the Annual General Meeting and secured the recognition thereof that the Board is Master of all things.

On the second day, it named the Chairman.

On the third day, it named the Secretary.

On the fourth day, it handed out the fees.

On the fifth day, it handed out the tokens of attendance.

214

On the sixth day, it chose the Managing Director and told him: 'Thou shalt labour in the sweat of thy brow.'

On the seventh, eighth and all subsequent days the Board, having completed its task, rested in peace.

It was right to do so; in the Managing Director it had made a good appointment.

At least the chairman was chosen on the second day and the board did fulfil one of its key functions, that of appointing the Managing Director.

APPENDIX 3

Hugh Parker has this to say about measuring board effectiveness in his *Letters to a New Chairman* (Director Publications, 1990):

> I have developed a check-list of six questions that I believe can be used by a chairman to test the effectiveness of his own board – and from that, as a starting-point, to decide what can be done to improve it.
>
> 1.   Has the board recently (or indeed ever) devoted significant time and serious thought to the company's longer-term objectives, and to the strategic options open to it for achieving them? If so, have these deliberations resulted in a board consensus or decision on its future objectives and strategies, and have these been put in writing?
>
> 2.   Has the board consciously thought about and reached formal conclusions on what is sometimes referred to as its basic 'corporate philosophy' – i.e. its value system, its ethical and social responsibilities, its desired 'image' and so forth? If so have these conclusions been codified or embodied in explicit statements of policy – for example, in respect of terms of employment, etc.? Does the company have formal procedures for recording and promulgating major board decisions as policy guidelines for down-the-line managers?
>
> 3.   Does the board periodically review the organisational structure of the company, and consider how this may have to change in future? Does it review and approve all senior appointments as a matter of course? Are adequate 'human resource development' programmes in place?
>
> 4.   Does the board routinely receive all the information it needs to ensure that it is in effective control of the company and its management? Have there been any 'unpleasant surprises' – for example, unfavourable results or unforeseen crises – that could be attributed to lack of timely or accurate information?

216

5.   Does the board routinely require the managing director to present his annual plans and budgets for their review and approval? Does the board regularly monitor the performance of the managing director and his immediate subordinate managers in terms of actual results achieved against agreed plans and budgets?

6.   When the board is required to take major decisions on questions of future objectives, strategies, policies, major investments, senior appointments etc., does it have adequate time and knowledge to make these decisions soundly – rather than finding itself overtaken by events and, in effect, obliged to rubber-stamp decisions already taken or commitments already made?

If the answers to all these questions are affirmative, it is safe to say that you have an effective board. If the answers are negative – or perhaps not clear – then you already have some indications of what needs to be done to strengthen your board.

BIBLIOGRAPHY

BOOKS

Beevor, J. G., *The Effective Board*, BIM Publications, 1975.
Brodie, M. B., *The Committee Concept and Business*, Administrative Staff College, 1963.
Brooks, J., *The Fate of the Edsel and Other Business Adventures*, Gollancz, 1964.
Bullock Report, Committee of Enquiry on Industrial Democracy, Cmd 6706, 1977.

CBI Company Affairs Committee, *The Responsibilities of the British Public Company*, CBI, 1973 (the Watkinson Report).
Charkham, J. P., *Effective Boards: The independent element and the role of the non-executive director*, Chartac Books, 1986.
Charkham, Jonathan, *Keeping Good Company*, Oxford University Press, 1994.
Clurman, Richard M., *Who's in Charge?*, Chief Executive Press, 1993.
Clutterbuck, David and Waine, Peter, *The Independent Board Director*, McGraw-Hill, 1994.

Demb, Ada and Neubauer, F.-Friedrich, *The Corporate Board*, Oxford University Press, 1992.
Drucker, P. D., *The Unseen Revolution*, Heinemann, 1976.

Friedman, Milton, *Capitalism and Freedom*, University of Chicago Press, 1982.

Harvey-Jones, Sir John, *Making It Happen*, Collins, 1988.
Heidrick and Struggles International, *The Role of the Chairman*, 1987.

Jay, Sir Antony, *Corporation Man*, Jonathan Cape, 1972.
Juran, J. M. and Louden, J. K., *The Corporate Director*, American Management Association Inc., 1966.

Koontz, Harold, *The Board of Directors and Effective Management*, McGraw-Hill, 1967.

Lessem, Ronnie and Neubauer, Fred, *European Management Systems*, McGraw-Hill, 1994.
Lindon-Travers, Ken, *Non-Executive Directors: Their role, responsibilities and appointment*, Director Books, 1990.

McKinsey and Co., *Effective Boardroom Management*, BIM Publications 1971.
Mills, Geoffrey, *Controlling Companies*, Unwin Hyman, 1988.
Monks, Robert A.G. and Minow, Nell, *Power and Accountability*, Harper Collins, 1994.

Parker, Hugh, *Letters to a New Chairman*, Director Publications, 1979, reprinted 1990.
Parkinson. Professor Northcote C., *Parkinson's Law*, John Murray, 1958.
Pastin, Mark, *Hard Problems of Management, Gaining the ethics edge*, Jossey Bass, 1986.
Puckey, Sir Walter, *The Board-Room*, Hutchinson, 1969.

Roberts, General Henry M., *Robert's Rules of Order*, Scott Foresman, revised 1981 edition.

Schoenberg, Robert J., *Geneen*, W.W. Norton, 1985.
Sloan, Alfred P., *My Years with General Motors*, Sidgwick and Jackson, 1986.

Tricker, R. I., *Corporate Governance*, Gower, 1984.

Watson Jr., Thomas J., *A Business and its Beliefs*, McGraw-Hill, 1963.
Wendt, Henry, *Global Embrace*, Harper Business, 1993.

BOOKLETS, ARTICLES AND SPEECHES

Allen, William T., Chancellor Delaware Court of Chancery, *Re-defining the role of outside directors*, April 1992.
Anglo-German Foundation, *The German Company*, 1993.

Baladi, André, 'Internationale Lobby für Institutioneller Anleger', *Handels-Zeitung*, May 1994.
BDO Binder Hamlyn, *Non-executive Directors – Watchdogs or Advisers?*, 1994.
Bosch, Henry, 'Corporate Practices and Conduct', *Information Australia*, 1993.
Bose, Mihir, 'Pearson's formula for growth', *Director*, September 1989.
Business Roundtable, *Corporate Governance and American Competitiveness*, March 1990.

Cabot, Louis W., 'On an effective board', *HBR (Harvard Business Review)*, Sept./Oct. 1976.

Charkham, J. P., 'Corporate governance and the market for the control of companies', Bank of England Panel Paper No. 25, March 1989.

Committee on the Financial Aspects of Corporate Governance, Gee, 1992.

Corby, Sir Brian, *Speech to the International Stock Exchange Conference*, November 1989.

Corporate Consulting Group, *Corporate Governance: The challenge for the chairman*, 1992.

Davis, Keith, 'Five propositions for social responsibility', *Business Horizons*, 1975.

Davison, Ian Hay, *The Developing Role of the Non-Executive Director*, ICSA, September 1991.

Dayton, K. N., 'Corporate governance', *HBR*, Jan./Feb. 1984.

Dixon, Stanley, 'The art of chairing a meeting', *Accountants Digest*, Winter 1975/76.

Drucker, Peter, 'The bored board', *Wharton Magazine*, 1976.

Drucker, Peter, 'The futures that have already happened', *The Economist*, 21 October 1989.

Egon Zehnder International, *Corporate Governance: The role of the non-executive director*, 1993.

Frankfurter Allgemeine Zeitung, *Aufsicht und Kontrolle*, February 1994.

General Motors' Guidelines on Significant Corporate Governance Issues, 1994.

Gilson, Ronald J. and Kraakman, Reinier, *Re-inventing the Outside Director*, Stanford University, June 1990.

Gilson, Ronald J. and Roe, Mark J., *Understanding the Japanese Keiretsu*, Stanford Law School, August 1992.

Governor of the Bank of England, 'The developing role and responsibilities of institutional shareholders', *Bank of England Quarterly Bulletin*, June 1986.

Henderson, Hazel, 'Should business tackle society's problems?', *HBR*, July/Aug. 1968.

Institute of Chartered Accountants, *The Private Investor and the Corporate Report*, 1978.

Institutional Shareholders' Committee, *The Role and Duties of Directors*, April 1991; *The Responsibilities of Institutional Shareholders in the UK*, December 1991.

Jensen, Michael C., 'Eclipse of the public corporation', *HBR*, Sept./Oct. 1989.

KPMG Peat Marwick, *Survey of Non-executive Directors*, 1994.

Lipton, Martin and Lorsch, Jay W., 'A modest proposal for improved corporate governance', *The Business Lawyer*, November 1992.

McFadzean, Lord, 'The key tasks of a company chairman', *International Management*, Jan. 1972.

National Association of Corporate Directors, *Performance Evaluation of Chief Executive Officers, Boards and Directors*, 1994.

Parker, Hugh, 'Creating tomorrow's chairman', *The Director*, 1990.
Parker, Hugh, *The Chairman of the Board*, Directors' Manual, 1990.
Parker, Hugh, 'The chairman/CEO separation', *Directors and Boards*, Spring 1994.
Patton, Arch and Baker, John, 'Why won't directors rock the boat?', *HBR*, Nov./Dec. 1987.
Peach, L. H., *IBM's Secondment Programme*, IBM (UK), 1983.
Pensions Investment Research Consultants, *Shareholder Voting Guidelines*, March 1994.
Point, Le, *Le Réseau Caché des Grands Patrons*, April 1994.

Rees-Mogg, Lord, 'The value of an outside voice in the drama of a takeover bid', *The Independent*, 12 September 1989.
RSA Enquiry, *Tomorrow's Company*, Interim Report, 1994.

Schneider-Lenné, Ellen R., *The Governance of Good Business*, Stockton Lecture, 1992.
Skapinker, Michael, 'Free lunches and privileged information', *The Financial Times*, 1 June 1987.
Stuttard, J. B. and Stanway, A. R., *Annual Corporate Reporting – the 1980's*, paper presented at Coopers & Lybrand's annual conference, 1978.

3i, *The Role and Contribution of an Independent Director*, Associate Directors Resources.
Tricker, R. I., *Chairman of the Board*, Corporate Policy Group, Oxford, 1981.
Tropman, John E., 'The effective committee chair: a primer', *Directors and Boards*, Summer 1980.

UK Shareholders' Association, *Bulletin*, Summer 1994.

van Sinderen, A. W., 'The Board looks at itself', *Directors and Boards*, Winter 1985.

Weekly Law Reports, *Byng v. London Life Association*, 28 April 1989.
Winning for Britain, Labour's strategy for success.

Woodstock, Stephen, *Corporate Governance in the Single European Market*, Royal Institute of International Affairs, 1990.

Working Group on Corporate Governance, 'A new compact for owners and directors', *HBR*, July/Aug. 1991.

INDEX

223